Out of the Shadow of 9/11

An Inspiring Tale of Escape and Transformation

Christina Ray Stanton

LOVING ALL NATIONS PRESS
NEW YORK, NEW YORK

For permission requests, write to the publisher at the address below:
Loving All Nations Press
150 Nassau Street, 4G
New York City, NY 10038
christinarstanton@gmail.com
christinaraystanton.com

Ordering Information:
Special discounts are available on quantity purchases by corporations, associations, and others.
For details, contact the publisher at the address above.

Project Manager: Marla Markman, MarlaMarkman.com
Editor: Tammy Ditmore, Editmore.com
Cover and Book Design: Kelly Cleary, kellymaureencleary@gmail.com

Publisher's Cataloging-in-Publication Data
Names: Stanton, Christina Ray, author.
Title: Out of the shadow of 9/11 : an inspiring tale of escape and transformation /
Christina Ray Stanton.
Description: New York, NY: Loving All Nations Press, 2019.
Identifiers: LCCN 2019902119 | ISBN 978-1-7337452-0-8 (pbk.) | 978-1-7337452-1-5 (ebook)
Subjects:
LCSH Stanton, Christina Ray. | September 11 Terrorist Attacks, 2001--Biography. |
Victims of terrorism--New York (State)--New York--Biography. |
Christian biography--United States. | September 11 Terrorist Attacks, 2001--
Religious aspects--Christianity. | World Trade Center (New York, N.Y.) |
Terrorism--United States. | BISAC BIOGRAPHY &AUTOBIOGRAPHY /
Personal Memoir | HISTORY / Modern / 21st Century |
Classification: LCC HV6432.7 .S736 2019 | DDC 973.931--dc23

978-1-7337452-0-8 (Softcover)
978-1-7337452-1-5 (eReaders)

Library of Congress Control Number: 2019902119

Printed in the United States of America

Dedication

I love you dearly, Brian. I'm the most blessed person
on the planet to have you.

Michelle Jennings and Sarah Anderson, thank you
for your incredible friendship.

To all three, thank you for helping me write this book!
I couldn't have done it without you.

Psalm 103:1: Let all that I am praise the Lord; with
my whole heart, I will praise his holy name.

Proceeds from this book will benefit Loving All Nations (lovingallnations.org),
which seeks to help the poor, vulnerable, and marginalized of the world.

Contents

Lord,

Take me where you want me to go,

Let me meet who you want me to meet,

Tell me what you want me to say and

Keep me out of your way.

—Father Mychal Judge (May 11, 1933–September 11, 2001)

1

Waking to a Nightmare:
September 11, 2001

"GET UP! GET UP!" Brian was shaking my arm forcefully and yelling. I had never heard that hint of panic in my husband's voice before.

"Someone's bombed the World Trade Center!"

Rubbing my eyes, I sat up and glanced at the clock: 8:46.

"What are you talking about? What's wrong?"

Brian was still shaking my arm, and one glimpse of the fear in his eyes jolted me fully awake.

He pointed toward the living room. "Come out on the terrace!"

I slid out of bed and followed him onto the terrace of our twenty-fourth-floor apartment. Thick black smoke was boiling up from the North Tower of the World Trade Center, six blocks away. The column of smoke stretched as wide as the building itself and rose high in the bright blue sky before being swept away by the wind.

The south side of the building, the one facing our apartment, looked totally fine. I couldn't make sense of it.

"It must be a bomb, Christina." Brian was talking so fast that I could barely understand him. "I bet someone snuck a suitcase bomb into the World Trade Center. I was sitting at my computer preparing for my upcoming job interviews when I heard a loud blast, then felt the vibration. You know how it feels when you're at a stop sign and the car next to you is playing really loud music and you can feel the bass thumping?" He hit his fist against his chest to demonstrate.

"Let's turn on the TV," I said, hurrying back inside. "I want to hear what Katie Couric is saying."

When I finally found the right channel, Katie was reporting: "We have a breaking news story to tell you about. Very little information is available, but it appears a plane has hit one of the Twin Towers."

"So, it wasn't a bomb," Brian said. "It was a small plane. How the heck did a plane fly into the tower?"

We flipped through the channels, searching for more information. But no TV report was as compelling as the scene unfolding right in front of our eyes. Returning to the terrace, we could tell that the fire had spread to the south side of the tower. The entire top of the tower was now engulfed in smoke. The smoke was so thick and dark that it barely looked real.

Dozens of emergency vehicles were racing toward the World Trade Center complex—lights flashing, sirens blaring. Fire trucks, police cars, and ambulances began blocking traffic on the West Side Highway, just below our building.

Brian stepped inside to catch the latest TV news report. "Hey, they are saying a commercial plane hit the tower—not a little one."

As I headed inside to hear the latest news, I noticed the clock: 8:56. Lots of people were probably just starting their day in one of the thousands of offices in the 110-floor building.

"I wonder if everyone knows about this. I'm going to call Mom and Michelle." I dialed Mom's number but hung up when I got her answering machine. I didn't want to spend time leaving a message, and I didn't know what to say anyway.

My friend Michelle answered after one ring.

"Michelle, turn on the TV," I commanded.

I heard her gasp. "Oh-my-gosh. . ." Her voice trailed off.

"I'm watching this from my balcony, but I wanted to make sure you knew this was going on!"

I hung up and rushed back to the terrace, looking from the expanding column of black smoke enveloping the tower to the chaos on the street below. Neither Brian nor I said anything. Suddenly, something caught my eye. Looking over my right shoulder, I saw a plane flying so low and so close that I wondered whether I would be able to see passengers looking out of its windows. With a thunderous, deafening roar, the jet swooped like a hawk between the buildings in front of us.

I screamed in terror as I watched the plane roll to the left until its wings were at about 8:00 and 2:00. With its nose aimed directly at the top of the South Tower, the plane was clearly *not* out of control.

We felt, rather than saw, the impact. One moment we were standing on the terrace, and the next we were lying on our backs in the middle of the living room floor. My ears were ringing, and a heavy weight on my chest pinned me to the ground. I opened my eyes to discover our forty-pound Boston terrier whimpering and panting in terror while jumping on my chest.

Pushing Gaby aside, I sat up and realized that Brian was speaking to me. I could hear his voice, but he seemed far away, and his words were jumbled. I tried to focus.

"Do you have your shoes on?"

I looked down at my bare feet.

"No."

I had no idea why shoes would matter. All I could think about was running away.

"Let's get out of here—hurry!"

I jumped up, ran through the front door, and rushed straight to the elevators in the hall. With my finger an inch away from the button, I froze, remembering the rule to never take elevators in emergencies. I hollered in the direction of our still-open door. "Let's take the stairs!"

From inside, Brian yelled, "Go ahead, I'll get Gaby's leash and bring him with me!" I opened the door to Staircase B and began my descent. I wasn't alone. Voices echoed throughout the stairwell.

"Did you see it? Did you see it?"

"This is horrible! I can't believe it. Are we under some kind of attack?"

I heard the fear in their voices, but I was lost in my own thoughts about the people in the towers and on the plane I had just seen streaking over my balcony.

Oh Lord, those poor people, those poor people, those poor people.

Reaching the street seemed to take forever. I counted every floor: nineteen, eighteen, seventeen, sixteen. I tried taking two stairs at a time while holding onto the railing, but I was becoming a bit dizzy. Finally, I could see the ground-floor door.

The woman in front of me held the emergency door open, and I followed her out to the busy street.

As my eyes adjusted to the sunlight, my mind attempted to adjust to the chaos. I put my hands over my ears, which had been hurting since the jet swooped past my balcony. Emergency vehicles sped by, their sirens momentarily drowning out shouts and screams from the people rushing past me. The people were all rushing south, away from the burning towers; the vehicles were all moving north.

Most people looked more bewildered than frightened, but a few appeared truly panicked—rushing blindly through the streets, unaware of anyone or anything else. Throngs of people were running across the West Side Highway, rushing directly into traffic, dodging cars, leaping over cement dividers. I had never seen anyone try to cross this major highway against traffic. Now, hundreds were.

I backed up against the side of my building to get out of the way of the torrent of people. I was facing away from the Twin Towers now, looking across the highway into Battery Park

City, where people were running haphazardly in all directions, searching desperately for the best escape route. I took a couple of cautious steps away from my apartment building and looked up at the sky. Pieces of paper were fluttering down like confetti.

The slamming of the emergency exit door brought me back to my senses. Neighbors were pouring out of my building, but Brian and Gaby weren't among them.

A wave of guilt washed over me. In my rush, I had panicked and just left them behind. Finally Brian burst out of the door, carrying Gaby over his shoulder.

"Where were you?" I snapped.

Sweaty and panting, Brian replied, "I had to carry Gaby down all those stairs!"

I realized then that carrying a forty-pound dog down twenty-four flights of stairs was no small feat, and my guilt intensified. Brian put Gaby on the ground and leashed him. He then stood up and looked around—his shocked expression mirrored my emotion.

We stood still for a minute, watching people running past us. Most of the men were wearing suits and ties, and the women were in blazers with matching pants or skirts. As I noticed a woman's designer outfit, I realized I had no idea what I was wearing. I looked down: a pink, sleeveless, knee-length cotton sundress that I used as a nightgown. No bra. No shoes.

I had noticed other people running down the stairwell in different stages of dress, but even then I had not taken time to consider what I was wearing. I had recurring nightmares about walking around undressed in a public place, and now here I was on a major Manhattan street in my PJs. I looked at Brian, and his black T-shirt, khaki shorts, and tennis shoes made me feel even more exposed.

"Brian, we gotta go back. I have to get some clothes and shoes on, and I need to get my purse too."

We turned around, but the emergency door was locked.

"I really don't want to climb twenty-four flights of stairs, anyway," Brian said. "Let's use the elevator."

We walked around the corner and through the revolving glass door. As we headed toward the elevators, Miguel, the doorman, stopped us.

"We're telling all the residents to evacuate the building; we need the elevators for people leaving. You can't go back upstairs."

"Miguel, I'm in my nightgown! I need to go back upstairs," I pleaded. In the two months we had lived in the building, I had seen Miguel go out of his way many times to please residents. But he was not budging now.

"Sorry, Christina. I can't let you do that. Everyone has to leave now."

Brian and I returned to the street. Standing barefoot on the sidewalk, watching people rush past with panic in their eyes, I realized that no one else was going to notice what I was or was not wearing this morning. But Brian *was* worried about my bare feet. "Here, wear my shoes," he said.

"No, no. Keep them, but let me wear your socks," I told him. Brian sat down, pulled off his thick, white, ankle-length socks, and handed them to me. I put them on and walked in a little circle to show him they would protect my feet. "These are fine," I told him.

Secretly, I prayed, "Lord, please let them be fine."

I began plotting our next move, relying on my years as a New York City tour guide to consider our options. We were on the southern tip of Manhattan island, and several roads led north, past the Financial District. But all of them would lead us right past the burning towers. I didn't want to go anywhere near that terrifying chaos, so our only option was to head south, to Battery Park.

We had taken Gaby on this four-minute walk to the park at the lower tip of the island almost every day since we had moved from North Carolina to Manhattan in July. Commuters routinely walk through the twenty-five-acre park to catch the Staten Island Ferry, while tourists routinely walk through it to catch sightseeing cruises to the Statue of Liberty. But nothing was routine today.

Panicked people rushed past us, running toward the park. Emergency vehicles screamed by in the other direction, heading toward the World Trade Center. Briefcases, books, eyeglasses, purses, and pieces of clothing littered the sidewalks and streets. I paused to pick up a pack of unopened cigarettes.

"I need a cigarette so, so badly right now," I said, marveling at my good fortune in finding a $9 pack of cigarettes on the ground.

"Christina," Brain scolded, "put that down. You don't know who those belong to!"

I stared at the cigarettes in my hand.

He's right. What's wrong with me? I never pick up stuff off the ground. What could I do with these, anyway—scour the ground for a lighter?!

Brian hadn't noticed the cigarettes because he was looking at the shoes scattered across the sidewalks and streets. "Look, Christina," he said. "I see at least fifty abandoned shoes!" Women's shoes, men's shoes, designer high heels, cheap athletic shoes. Some were in pairs; others had been dropped with no mate in sight.

"Brian, do you think the shoes were blown out of the Towers? Or the planes?"

"I doubt it," he said. "I'm guessing that people just ran off in a panic. If they couldn't run in their shoes, they left them behind. Or they threw away anything they had been carrying."

Marveling that people could get so panicked that they would leave their shoes behind, Brian and I walked on, never considering for a second that I could look for a pair of shoes that might fit me.

I could still see smoke billowing upward and spreading across the entire area. The smoke continued to grow thicker, and it was hovering like a dark cloud over the alley where we were standing—nine blocks away. Paper and scraps floated through the air around us and piled up on the ground like snowdrifts.

My ears pulsed with the constant sirens from ambulances looping into Battery Place and then onto the West Side Highway toward the burning towers. Brian tightened his grip on Gaby's leash and then grabbed my hand. We took a deep breath and stepped off the curb when we saw a small break in the line of cars. Hopscotching through traffic, we tried to stay together as we dodged ambulances and fire trucks; Gaby stuck like a shadow to Brian's side. Finally we broke through the last lane of traffic and stumbled into the haven of Battery Park.

2

A Safe Haven Becomes a Death Trap

BREATHING A SIGH OF RELIEF, we joined a crowd who had gathered on the half-moon sidewalk bordering the top of the park and turned to see what was happening in the neighborhood we had just escaped. A stream of people was rushing straight toward us from the Financial District. Some walked slowly, as if they could barely lift their feet. Others sprinted frantically. Many held purses and briefcases over their heads to shield themselves from falling debris. All frequently looked over their shoulders to catch glimpses of the burning towers.

The edge of the park had been transformed into the finish line of a marathon. When people stepped out of the street, their expressions changed from determination and fear to relief. Some stopped as soon as they hit the concrete sidewalk, putting their hands on their hips or bending over to catch their breath. Others collapsed onto benches or the grass. A few fumbled through their pockets for phones. Watching their relief made me feel better—I desperately wanted to believe that the worst was over.

They're safe now. We're all safe.

About a hundred people were on the sidewalk around us, with more arriving every moment. As soon as the new arrivals caught their breath, they joined the rest of us—staring at the burning buildings to our north. For the first time since we had left our terrace, Brian and I could see both towers clearly. From street level, the towers appeared even taller and more formidable, but we could see that long columns of black smoke had engulfed the buildings, which each stood a quarter mile high. The smoke from each tower joined together and drifted east in one huge black cloud. Wind spread the ominous mass across the sky, carrying with it a strange smell of paint thinner, wood, and burning plastic and rubber.

Am I still asleep? Is this just a nightmare? I'm in Battery Park. My Battery Park. I've walked Gaby here, I've brought scores of tourists here, much less all the other time I've spent here in the past eight years. How can this be happening?

I felt a need to find something familiar, something constant.

"Honey, do you have a phone? I want to try to call Mom."

"I left them in the apartment. I forgot them," Brian said, looking dismayed.

"Briaaannnnnn . . ." I wailed, flashing him an angry look. "How could you forget our phones?"

"We were in a *hurry*, Christina!" More gently, he added, "You forgot a few things too."

I looked down at my nightgown with a jolt. "Oh yeah," I said sheepishly, ashamed of how I had just snapped at my husband.

Here I am getting on his case, and—hello—I left my phone, purse, and even my shoes!

~

We were still standing shoulder to shoulder with the growing crowd of people who had fled to Battery Park. Feeling a little safer, I started to pay more attention to the people around me. Many were fiddling with their phones, but few seemed to be talking on them.

"Is your cell phone working?" a skinny man in a suit asked.

"No!" several people shouted in unison.

One man yelled, "Mine is. I just found out that a plane hit the Pentagon in DC!"

Brian and I looked at each other in shock. People started shouting or moaning. "We're at war!" "We're being attacked!"

Rumors flew from every direction.

"A plane went down in Times Square!"

"One hit the United Nations!"

"A plane is on its way to take down the Statue of Liberty!"

"Oh my God, Brian," I said, fighting a rising sense of fear and despair.

"Let's get away from this crowd," Brian said quietly.

He pointed south toward the water, and we started walking. We followed the route I usually took with Gaby, passing the Korean War monument and heading toward the Mariner's Memorial in the New York Harbor. Neither one of us said much, but my mind was racing to unpredictable destinations.

Is every landmark getting attacked? Is anywhere safe? Will anything be left of Manhattan?

What about the rest of the country? What about Mom? She's probably safe in Tallahassee, right? But I bet she's worried about me!

I wish I had brought my camera. Someday, I might want pictures of what this hell looked like.

At the water's edge, we sat on a bench facing the harbor, turning our backs to the burning towers and panicked crowds. Only a handful of people had made it this far across the park, and we were relieved to have a quiet space to collect ourselves. Gaby sat on the concrete in front of us, shaking with fear. I stared at the Statue of Liberty, praying that I wouldn't see a plane crash into it.

I fought the temptation to turn and see what was happening to the Twin Towers. Although it was hard not to stare at the billowing smoke cloud, it felt almost immoral to watch. Voyeuristic. But I couldn't stop thinking about what was happening behind me. How many tourists had I led to those buildings in the years I worked as a tour guide? My memorized spiel came back to me in a flash:

"Here are some fun facts about the Twin Towers: 47,000 people work there. The buildings encompass twelve million square feet of office space. The observation deck receives 1.8 million visitors a year—as many as 10,000 per day. Each floor is the equivalent of one acre. The complex houses more than 430 companies from twenty-eight countries. It cost one billion dollars to create. There are 40,000 doorknobs....."

Forty-seven-thousand people. How many were there when the planes hit? Are they trapped? How many have died already? Is it in the hundreds? Thousands? Were there tour groups on the observation deck?

I couldn't bring myself to watch the burning buildings because it felt like watching someone drown when you don't know how to swim. All you can do is stand at the water's edge while they suffer.

There was another reason I couldn't look, which frightened me even more. I felt an overwhelming sense of evil around us and in the billowing smoke. Watching the towers burn was like looking directly into the face of that evil force. It made my skin crawl.

Brian and I stayed on the bench. We didn't speak, and I put my fingers in my ears to drown out the crowd and the screaming sirens. The water was so peaceful and the sky directly in front of us was free of smoke. Looking straight ahead, I could almost pretend that nothing unusual was happening at all.

Eventually, Brian and I decided to walk back to our apartment. We could tell from here that the fire had not spread into our neighborhood—maybe they would at least let us back in to get our things? We stood up and headed north. As we neared the entrance to Battery Park, the ground began to shake violently. A thunderous noise filled my already aching ears.

I froze, terrified.

Suddenly, even though I could see nothing, I knew what was happening.

"Brian, a tower is coming down!"

There was no warning, no build-up. It had never crossed my mind that it was even possible for a tower to collapse. No one sharing scary rumors in the Battery Park crowd had speculated that a tower might fall. I strained to see the towers but saw only trees and smoke. But my ears told me the building was toppling over—and falling toward us. We were not safe at all!

The park erupted into panic and pandemonium. The people who had been watching the towers burn turned and began running toward us, screaming in terror. The hysterical crowd broke into clumps as runners flew down the meandering trails, which suddenly became a giant obstacle course. Dodging trees and stone monuments, runners hurdled over bushes and catapulted over waist-high fences. Everyone was headed south.

When they saw water dead ahead, terrified runners either sank to the ground in despair or switched directions and continued to run in an aimless, senseless hysteria. I was petrified and paralyzed. At times, I felt like I was hovering above the scene, watching myself and the panicked crowd in slow motion.

An Asian businessman in a tattered expensive suit sprinted past me, clutching his briefcase, his face contorted in agony. A woman with a German shepherd rushed past, holding the leash waist-high. A woman running in the opposite direction hit the leash and flipped over it, landing hard. The dog owner paused to tend to her.

About ten women wearing hotel chambermaid uniforms darted in all directions, screaming at the top of their lungs. Their short-sleeved brown dresses, white collars, and white cuffs marked them as employees from the Marriott World Trade Center.

Brian and I stood in a stationary haze. I had never before witnessed anyone fighting for their life, and this terrified me more than the burning towers, more than the noise and the smoke that began permeating the air. Seeing the fear of death on the faces of the people around me caused me to completely shut down.

A man ran past us to the harbor and leapt over the bannister at the edge of the park, apparently getting ready to dive into the deep water.

Tugging on Brian's shirt, I asked, "Hey, what do you think? Could we swim it?" We looked across New York Harbor. Staten Island was in the distance but New Jersey, Governor's Island, and Brooklyn seemed closer.

"Governor's Island is probably a mile away," Brian said. "I'm not sure we could swim that far. Gaby certainly couldn't."

"You're right. Let's not try it."

But seeing the man getting ready to swim away jolted me out of my stupor. Panic shot through me as the falling tower avalanche continued to thunder. "We need to get outta here!"

Brian and I joined a stream of people running along a path leading east, and I realized we were headed toward the terminal to the Staten Island Ferry. We sprinted to keep up but found ourselves at the tail end of a crowd bottlenecking at the glass entrance doors. As the thunderous sound behind us began to diminish, I fervently hoped we had found our escape route.

But as we neared the doors, a chorus of screams rose like a wave in front of me. Two large white lights were coming straight for us through the smoke, and someone began screaming, "It's another plane. It's another plane!" The crowd wheeled around and began running in a panic. We ran too, until the sound of a foghorn stopped us in our tracks. It wasn't another plane—it was just the Staten Island ferry coming in to dock. Our panic had caused us to run away from the very vessel we had been hoping would carry us away from this nightmare.

Clearly, we needed to get ourselves together. We abandoned the idea of getting into the Staten Island terminal and decided to concentrate on getting out of the aggressive smokey air streams that had materialized. My rational and logical husband looked up and noticed the smoke stream was blowing east and south, so he decided we should walk west and north.

After a few minutes, we stopped to catch our breath and see

if we were in the clear. We looked back just as the smoke stream engulfed the entire terminal. In seconds a horde of people emerged from the smoke—stampeding in our direction. We turned and started sprinting, fearing the crazed crowd would run us over.

Situated at the front of the pack, we kept running west until Brian suddenly veered north toward the old Castle Clinton fort. I followed closely, knowing he was trying to steer us clear of the crowd. Many people continued running west, a few ran south, but no one else was running north. North was the direction of the danger. My own inner alarm started clanging, and I fought every instinct in my body so I could follow my husband.

Brian stopped at the northwest side of the fort. We hugged its circular wall, trying to catch our breath and calm down. Gaby flopped on the ground, exhausted. Only then did I realize how exhausted I was. Feeling overwhelmed, I focused on coming to my senses so I could make rational decisions.

Deep breaths, girl, take deep breaths. Get ahold of yourself. Need to think straight. There's gotta be something we can do to get out of this madness.

But every time I tried to take a deep breath, I inhaled soot and the sickening scent of burning electrical wiring. I couldn't block out the shrieks and cries of people who believed they were about to die, and I couldn't ignore the people running aimlessly all around me. As far as I could see, Brian and I were the only ones standing still. We turned toward each other. I searched his face but could not tell what he was thinking. Nothing in our eighteen months of marriage had prepared us for this madness.

"Brian, is this it? Are we gonna die?"

He hesitated, then looked me in the eye. "I don't know. Maybe," he said sadly.

As we stood there in the shadow of the fort, Brian took my hands and began praying aloud: "Our Father, who art in heaven, hallowed be thy name, thy kingdom come, thy will be done. . . ."

As he recited the Lord's Prayer, I began my own silent entreaty. *Lord, I'm worried about mother. Please watch over her if I die. Lord, I'm sorry I've spent lots of time doing life without you. That I haven't been serious in my relationship with you. I'm sorry I haven't been a better daughter. Please forgive me for my anger and stubbornness. I'm sorry I've held grudges.*

I looked up as Brian continued to pray, and gratitude replaced my fears.

Brian and I will be together, whatever happens. I'm so glad I'm with him now. God, you gave me such a wonderful gift, this awesome man. I have great friends. I love you, God. Thank you, God, for being with me throughout my life. I'm a very blessed woman. I've lived a very blessed life. I even got to live in the city of my childhood dreams.

I opened my eyes. My dream city was now a hellscape.

3

Concentrating on Surviving

A COMMUNAL SHRIEK rose from the park, and I knew something horrible was coming our way. Before we could move, a mass of *something* hit me in the face while a gust of wind flung the bottom of my nightgown up around my waist. I staggered several feet southward before the gust died down as quickly as it came. I felt as if someone had thrown a bucket of sticky sand over me: gunk filled my nose and mouth and coated every pore of unprotected skin.

I opened my eyes slowly, trying to protect them from whatever was on my eyelids. Brian hadn't moved, but he looked completely different—like an upright mummy. The entire landscape was now a grayish yellow color. Everything. The trees, the grass, the shrubs, the ground, the statues, the people, their clothes.

It looks like we're on the moon!

Particles hovered thick in the air, and a grayish yellow ceiling suspended over us, trapping us like specimens in a terrarium. The yellow gunk was filmy and sticky. I picked some off my arm and tried to identify the strange texture—it wasn't as gritty as sand, or as thick as snowflakes, or as thin as pollen. It resembled ashes from a wood fire—yellow ashes. But this ash didn't continue to fall to the ground when it hit my body. It stuck to me. The sticky substance was continuing to fall, adding layer upon layer on my skin and my surroundings.

"Agh! What is this? Where'd it come from?" I sputtered, spitting out gunk.

"I think it's the tower," Brian speculated.

We quit trying to talk because every time we opened our mouth we sucked in the falling sludge. All morning, we had been awash in a sea of noise: a jet screaming overhead, sirens, traffic, screams, thunderous roars. Now, it was silent. Completely silent. People weren't talking. The roaring had stopped. We couldn't even hear sirens or any hint of traffic moving.

With every breath, I inhaled more of the sticky stuff. I cupped my hands over my nose and mouth but that only filtered out part of it.

I lifted the neckline of my nightgown over my nose. It made a crappy filter because it was so thin that the ash had permeated it completely, but it was my only option. I was still breathing in the filth, but by pressing my lips together I could keep from swallowing it. Brian pulled his shirt over his mouth and nose, too. Gaby was shaking violently, like he did after his bath, trying in vain to throw off the gunk sticking to his body. I didn't know how to help him.

No one was running anymore. People just sat or milled slowly and aimlessly like silent, yellow, walking zombies. There was nowhere to go. We were trapped like lab rats in a world covered in sticky yellow granules. I saw someone lying face up on the ground, not moving, as a man crouched over the form, crying. Completely covered in yellow, the body looked like the body casts of Pompeii victims I had seen once while traveling through Italy.

I wondered vaguely if the person was dead, but I felt no shock or horror or even sadness. I had become detached. Analytical. I no longer felt any emotions.

Brian steered me and Gaby toward Pier A with one hand while holding his shirt over his nose and mouth with the other. In a muffled voice he said, "Let's move up the coastline. I'm sure everything north of the West Side Highway is a no-go—the tower probably fell in that direction and cut off that route. We can't go east because the smoke stream's pouring over the park and it's still strong. But maybe if we stick to the Battery Park Esplanade we can walk our way out of this."

I nodded.

I followed Brian up the waterfront. We passed the rotting Pier A at the northwestern edge of Battery Park and crossed into Wagner Park, where the promenade picks up again. As we passed out of one park into another, a gust of wind kicked up, rerouting the smoke stream toward the southwest. The shift sparked another stampede of people trying to escape the smoke, a constantly shifting threat to everyone still in Battery Park.

In Wagner Park, the ceiling of yellow dust began dissipating, and the beautiful weather of the day reemerged. Still, we kept moving. Although the air seemed clearer here, all the people we passed were still covering their faces with anything they had. A young woman sat alone, crying hysterically. I felt no sympathy— only impatience.

What is she doing? There's plenty of time to cry later. She needs to do what we all need to do right now. She's not being practical, and she's making the situation worse for herself!

We kept walking.

Up ahead, one man was yelling at another. "Put that damn thing down right now, man!"

A young guy clutched a camera to his torso defensively.

Although I had earlier wished for my own camera, the angry man made me realize there was something distasteful about photographing this scene. This was not an event to be captured like a souvenir from an exotic vacation.

"Honey, let's walk faster," I said. I wanted to be away from these angry men, away from burning and falling towers, away from dust clouds and panicked crowds.

Near the Jewish Heritage Museum, which sits close to the

shore of the Hudson River, we saw about fifty people who had gathered around two large weeping willow trees.

"Let's wait here with this crowd," Brian said. "Maybe they have heard help is coming. Or maybe they stopped because the esplanade up ahead is blocked."

Brian and I sat down on the lawn near one of the willows, which I had always loved. Today, sticky yellow grime covered their long branches, making them look like ghoulish Halloween decorations.

My eyes felt prickly, like they were filled with tiny splinters, but I was afraid to rub them—afraid of what might be in the dust, on my hands, on my clothes. Since the ash-dust was settling, I felt myself starting to unwind just a bit.

Suddenly a dust-caked man appeared, yelling and waving his arms as he ran toward us. "The second building is coming down! Run to the river and turn your backs to it!"

We leapt to our feet and ran the few feet to the bank of the Hudson, crouching low to the ground next to a curved railing. The second tower—we later learned this was the North Tower—collapsed with another thunderous roar, but it didn't seem as violent as the first fall. Or maybe it just felt less violent because we had been warned. Or because we'd already been through the experience. We hunkered down, waiting for the fallout—for the cloud of gunk and dust—but it never came, although we witnessed a sky-high plume of it directly east. Slowly, we realized that the second tower must have fallen away from our position.

I noticed Gaby licking his fur, desperately trying to clean himself. "Stop, Gaby!" I pushed his head to the side, certain that he should not be ingesting whatever was in the gunk coating his body.

For the first time, I realized how obedient our typically stubborn dog had been all morning. He had behaved perfectly on the leash for the first time in his life. He ran when we ran, stopped when we stopped, and walked right by our side when we walked. He had not barked or whined or tried to gain our attention at any point since we left the apartment. The poor guy had clearly absorbed everyone's panic and fear and appeared as petrified as the humans. I felt a bit guilty that I hadn't paid more attention to him during this nightmare. But concentrating on our own survival was the best thing we could do for him. Somehow, he seemed to realize that too.

Suddenly, some of the people who'd been crouched by the railing near us stood up and began yelling and waving their arms at firefighting boats that were racing up the river.

"Over here!"

"We need help!"

"Please! Come get us!"

No one on the boats seemed to notice.

I began pondering escape routes. In normal times, a short walk up the coastline would take us to the neighborhood of Tribeca. We could just walk north and be free. Of course, that route would also take us just a few blocks west of the World Trade Center—or what was left of it. I risked tasting more yellow gunk to ask Brian his opinion.

"Do you think we could walk on the esplanade past the Winter Garden, to Stuyvesant High School, and then get out of this?"

"If it was an option, there'd be a stream of people doing just that right now," Brian replied. "It would be a big waste of energy if it was a dead end."

My anxiety began to grow again, along with a new, deeper level of desperation. I knew the Twin Towers had both collapsed—something that had been unimaginable only a few hours ago—and I had no idea what other unimaginable events might be happening just beyond our little tip of the island. We had heard that other buildings had been hit and that the Statue of Liberty was in jeopardy. I began to wonder if landmarks had crumbled all over New York City. What had happened to the Brooklyn Bridge, the Empire State Building, the Chrysler Building, Wall Street?

We were hemmed in by smoke, the burning ruins of the towers, and the Hudson River, with filthy dust thick in the air as far as the eye could see. I sank back to the ground by the railing. "We're trapped, Brian. We're really trapped."

4

A Boat Lift to New Jersey

ABOUT THIRTY PEOPLE HAD GATHERED near us by the railing along the river, and we were all watching the fireboats that continued to pass. Cries for help had deteriorated into profanity-laced tirades. A businessman with torn pants and a bloodied shirt yelled, "Come over here and *fucking* get us!" at every boat that passed. For most of the people in the crowd, anger had replaced fear, and the swearing man was stoking it to a fever pitch.

"The boat captains are neglecting us!"

"Can't they see we need help, damn it?"

I sympathized with the desperation of the people around me, but I was ready to get away from this increasingly angry crowd. Looking around, I noticed another group of people about thirty feet away who were forming a line by the railing.

"Brian, look over there. Maybe those people are organizing something?"

I looked back at the Hudson and recognized the outline of a tugboat coming closer and closer. The tugboat approached the railing, and ropes were thrown to men waiting at the railing.

"C'mon, Christina!" Brian grabbed my hand and we rushed to get in the line. As we reached it, however, I quickly realized that the boat was way too small to take everyone who was waiting. As the tugboat backed up and left, I tried to reassure Brian—and myself—that we had not missed our only chance.

"This can't be it, Brian! I'll bet that tugboat got on the radio and told others that there was a pile of people here waiting to board boats."

I was confident enough to stay in the queue, but as the tugboat disappeared, I sank down the railing and sat on the concrete, preparing for a long wait. To my surprise, I saw an outline of another boat approaching almost immediately. It was a large white New York Waterway, a ferry boat that travels between Manhattan and New Jersey.

"Christina, we will probably all fit on this one!" Brian grabbed my hands to help me back up.

Relief flooded over me, and I hollered, "YES! Thank you, Lord! Woohoo!"

Ropes were flung over the railing and the boat secured, but as I neared the front of the line, I was shocked by what I saw. The boat had not pulled up to a wharf or pier or any semblance of a normal boat dock—just a pedestrian walkway behind a four-foot railing built to keep people from falling into the Hudson. The deck of the boat was about seven feet below the top of the seawall, and the railing towered over the boat. There did not appear to be a ladder or ramp in sight. My tour-guide training had taught me to emphasize safety at all times—especially in New York's lawsuit-happy environment—and I knew this was no way to safely load a boat.

"Someone's gonna get hurt in this crazy loading process. And then they're gonna sue," I declared to Brian.

As we neared the boarding spot, I saw that two muscular men in the short-sleeved shirts worn by dockhands on the Statue of Liberty ferries had taken charge of the loading process. They had developed an unorthodox system that would never have been accepted in normal times—manually picking up people and lowering them into the boat or helping others jump or climb down on their own. It was awkward and slow, but these two men were making it work.

The line of people in front of us seemed to go on forever. I stopped worrying about how the boat was being loaded because all I could think about was escaping.

Nothing matters but getting away from here. Nothing.

Finally, it was our turn. Brian was in front of me carrying Gaby. A deckhand in the boat raised his arms, pointed to himself, and indicated silently that he intended to catch Gaby. He yelled up to Brian, "Hey, does that dog bite?"

His words caught me off guard and made me mad. I was too confused to figure out why he had even asked the question. Brian, unperturbed, yelled back, "No, he doesn't bite," before half-lowering, half-tossing Gaby to the man below. Gaby must have felt as confused as I did because he docilely accepted this rough treatment. Despite Brian's reassurances, our dog normally *would* bite when he felt threatened; thankfully, the deckhand did not learn of Gaby's mean streak.

The guys helped me get into a seated position on the curved railing, my legs dangling over the edge. They gave me a few seconds to balance myself before lowering me toward the deck.

"Hey man, watch the lady's skirt," one of them said to the other.

The comment just confused me. "I'm not wearing a skirt," I thought. "And why is he worried about anybody's skirt at a time like this?" My overloaded brain could not register that the man was simply concerned about keeping my nightgown-dress from riding up.

The guys took my forearms and eased me down. I looked up to see Brian climbing over the railing and jumping into the boat without help. The man handed Gaby back to Brian. Finally, we all were on board.

"Where is this boat going?" Brian asked.

"Paulus Hook. New Joisey."

⁓

"Brian, follow me." I had been on many boats like this one in my years as a New York City tour guide, so I led the way through interior passageways, up a short staircase to the open-air deck, and toward the spot where tourists could get the best photos of the Statue of Liberty. I saw about 200 evacuees both below deck and up top—office employees, women in workout clothes, parents with kids and babies in tow.

Some looked as if it was a regular morning—their clothing clean and untouched. Others were like us, covered with yellow dust, ragged and disheveled. A few were bloody, their clothes shredded. I tried not to stare at a blood-soaked man whose clothes seemed to have more gaping holes than material. He was sitting alone, staring straight ahead as if in shock.

Maybe the ones who look worse than us were in the towers when the planes hit? Or just close enough to the towers to be hit by debris?

Many of the people who had been picked up from the shore were crying, and several wore the wide-eyed panicked look I had been seeing all morning. Others had slipped into that impassive expression practiced by every New Yorker. No one was talking. Brian and I sank onto a bench, and he picked up Gaby and put him on his lap. It felt so good to sit down.

The boat pushed off about ten minutes later. As we set out, I could see dozens of boats of all shapes and sizes approaching Battery Park and Battery Park City, the residential neighborhood just above the park. They were coming from every direction— New Jersey, Brooklyn, Staten Island, Long Island. I saw Circle Line sightseeing vessels, NY Waterway ferry boats, dinner cruise ships, tugboats. I knew all the boats were headed to pick up people trapped on the southern tip of Manhattan.

Are there enough people to fill all those boats? Or maybe they're trying to evacuate everyone out of Manhattan. That makes sense to me. Get all 1.5 million people out of Manhattan until things stabilize. What might be next, an atomic bomb?

I turned toward the downtown Manhattan skyline. A cloudy dust blob enclosed the Twin Towers—or the spot where they once had stood—and stretched beyond the end of Battery Park out into the harbor. From this angle, the dust took on a white hue, not the yellow shade we had been seeing from inside the ashy snow globe. The dust cloud was interrupted at various points by streams of thick black smoke. A tall building or two would suddenly be visible, only to be concealed again by the dust clouds being blown south.

I turned away, troubled by the sense of immoral voyeurism I had felt earlier—coupled now with guilt. I knew there were people within those clouds that covered Lower Manhattan; people covered in gunk, waiting for boats, dodging the smoke, running around in a yellow terrarium trying to find a way to safety. And I knew I could do nothing to help them.

I got up and walked around the top level of the boat, stopping in disbelief when I came across a clock: 11:50. Just three hours since Brian had shaken me awake. Three hours of sheer terror that had seemed like three lifetimes.

But we were alive! And sailing away from Armageddon.

That's all that mattered.

5

Refugees—American Style

As I stood looking at the clock, I realized I was incredibly thirsty and hungry. I hadn't eaten anything all day, and inhaling and ingesting smoke and dust and gunk and running who knows how many miles had left me parched in a way I had never experienced. Brian and Gaby must be hungry and thirsty, too. I started off to look for something to eat or drink but realized I had no money.

I walked back to Brian. "I need to get some water. Do you have any cash?" He handed me two dollar bills.

Thank you, Lord, that my husband remembered to grab his wallet before running down the stairs! What if neither one of us had ID, credit cards, or cash?

I was dismayed to discover that the concession stand was closed, so I made my way to the bathroom, cupped my hands under the faucet and drank a few handfuls, ignoring the large sign claiming the water was "Unfit For Drinking." I wanted desperately to wash my gritty eyes, but concluded I could never do a proper job with no paper towels or real mirrors while on a boat moving through choppy waters. I might only make things worse. Still hungry, thirsty, and gritty, I returned to the top deck.

Thankfully, our ride across the Hudson River lasted only about ten minutes.

"Do you know where Paulus Hook is?" I asked Brian.

"Never heard of it."

I hoped desperately that Paulus Hook would offer a place to get something to eat, access to a bathroom, and a store where I could get some shoes.

When the boat docked at a shabby-looking pier, I found I didn't want to stand up.

"Let me sit a bit longer—I'm so tired," I said to Brian.

"OK, I understand."

The three of us were among the last to leave the boat. We headed toward a woman in uniform stationed at the end of the old wooden pier, assuming she would help us. Passengers ahead of us were speaking with her and then fanning out in different directions. When we approached, I asked, "Is there any place that can help us refugees?"

I was surprised and slightly embarrassed that I had used that word, although it seemed appropriate. But it seemed to irritate the woman, who replied sarcastically, *"Refugees? There are no refugees here!* No, there's nothing like that going on."

She might as well have said, "What's wrong with you, Drama Queen? You're here. You're fine. Don't be a wuss. Go on about your business."

She turned her head to indicate the conversation was done. I felt my cheeks grow hot. As we walked away, I thought of all the things I should have said to her. I fought the urge to turn back and say, "Do you know what we just went through? We. Are. Not. Fine."

Instead, Brian and I just kept walking, trying to figure out what to do next.

"There's a group pooling over there," Brian said, pointing to a small clump of people who had been on our boat. We walked toward them and Brian called out, "Hey, does anyone know what's near here?"

A woman answered, "I'm from this area. There's a shopping plaza and a mall nearby—about a mile or so away. You can walk with us—that's where we're headed."

We joined the group and made our way through streets filled

with generic-looking glass office buildings. I didn't see a bodega, restaurant, or a pharmacy. The businesses appeared closed; the sidewalks and streets were empty. As we approached a set of railroad tracks, I remembered my socked feet for the first time in hours.

"Brian, I'm worried about where I'll be stepping. I'll bet there's broken glass and nails and stuff around the tracks," I fretted. I sat down and took off the formerly white socks, which were now completely black. "Why don't you piggy-back for this part? I'll get you over the tracks," Brian said.

We crossed the tracks and walked for another quarter mile before we arrived in a more residential neighborhood. It was a beautiful day; the weather was mid-seventies and sunny, without a cloud in the sky. The town was peaceful and quiet. Totally unharmed.

Set against this bucolic scene, the fifteen of us in tattered clothes covered in yellow dust looked like characters out of a zombie movie. The area was quiet, and the group walked silently. Small talk felt inappropriate, and we were bone weary. We just wanted to find an office, a store, a restaurant, a phone—something.

Until my need for a bathroom began to outweigh everything else.

"Brian, I've got to go. Now. Can we see if there's a bathroom in those buildings over there?"

Brian nodded, and we peeled away from the group. We approached the residential complex and searched for a lobby or a community center, but all the main doors were locked. I *really* had to go. I prepared to go in the bushes, although that made me feel subhuman.

Lord, PLEASE help me here. This just sucks. Please help me find a bathroom.

Just then, a woman about my age walked by with a plastic

shopping bag. She looked us up and down and then asked, "Can I help you? Are you looking for something?"

Knowing what we looked like, I was surprised that this woman had even spoken to us. "I need to use the bathroom badly, ma'am. Do you know where I can find one?"

She answered, "I live in this complex. You can certainly use my bathroom. What are your names?"

"Brian and Christina," my husband answered. "We're from Manhattan, and we witnessed the attacks."

She responded sincerely and earnestly, "I figured you did. It must have been awful. I'm so sorry. I'm Anna, by the way. You are very welcome to come up to my place for anything you need right now." She keyed us into her lobby and together we rode the elevator.

Brian asked, "Anna, where are we? What town are we in?"

"You're near Hamilton Park in the Newport/Pavonia area."

I couldn't believe anyone would invite strangers up to their apartment, especially filthy strangers with a mangy dog. But this woman clearly wanted to help us.

As we got off the elevator and followed her down the hall, I whispered to Brian excitedly, "She was sent to help us. This is no coincidence." He nodded and smiled.

A man was watching the news on TV in the apartment. Anna said, "David, I just ran into these people downstairs. They were mixed up with what happened at the World Trade Center."

"Oh my God! Wow, no way. Really? How are you guys?" David said, getting up to shake our hands.

He looked shocked, as if he were seeing ghosts. I'm sure we did look like some sort of yellow specters, me standing there in my nightgown and socks, both of us covered by a thick layer of ashy dust. David had been sitting, watching scenes of Lower Manhattan on TV, when manifestations of the horror appeared in the flesh right in his living room. I made a beeline to the bathroom.

When I came out, I heard Brian saying, "Thank you so much for your hospitality. Sorry to ask for more, but can we use your phone?"

"We've been trying to use it all morning," Anna replied. "Sometimes we'll get a busy signal, sometimes there's not even that. You won't be able to get through to anyone. We've tried."

Anna brought us some water, which we sucked down eagerly. Then she set out a bowl of water for Gaby, who did the same. We stood for a few minutes longer, watching the TV coverage. Although we both were exhausted and starved for information, we didn't want to sit down because we were so filthy.

I had been completely apathetic to my physical appearance for the past four hours, but I suddenly became painfully aware that I was in a flimsy nightgown, braless, and shoeless. I turned beet red, though I'm sure the yellow film on my face prevented Anna and David from seeing that. I felt totally indecent in this setting untouched by the destruction, as if I had been thrust back into reality after leaving a surreal world.

I looked at Brian and could tell he felt the same.

"Thank you so much for everything," I said hastily. "We'll never forget this kindness. We really have to be going."

"Are you sure?" she replied. "You can stay as long as you want!"

"You are so sweet to offer, but we really need to go." I didn't know where we were going—I just wanted so much to get to a comfortable place where we could get all our needs met without feeling like aliens.

As we backed out of the apartment, I said a quick prayer: *Lord, thank you so much for bringing that woman to us! Thank you for that gift!*

Leaving the apartment, Brian and I headed toward the commercial district and were delighted to find a BJ's wholesale club, although I was a little worried that we would not be allowed in the store because we didn't have a membership card.

"Surely they'll let us use their bathroom!" Brian said. Feeling like we were approaching an oasis after a crawl across the desert, we began running toward the entrance. As we got closer, we saw yellow-caked people sitting or lying around the front of the store and the small islands of grass and trees interspersed throughout the parking lot. Some were eating sandwiches and snack food. A few were crying. A handful were sleeping. At least fifty people were lined up at a phone booth in front of the store.

Like us, these people obviously had no idea where to go or what to do. I didn't care what that official at the New Jersey pier had said. This was a refugee camp—American-style.

We walked through a set of sliding doors, and Gaby and I waited while Brian talked to the store greeter. "We don't have a membership card. Can we bring our dog into the store? Can we use your bathroom? Can we purchase items?"

"No, we don't allow pets in the building, but you are welcome to use our bathroom and you'll be able to buy items without a card today," the greeter replied.

"Let's switch off," Brian said to me. "One stays outside with Gaby while the other goes into the store. Do you mind if I'm first? I'll be as quick as I can."

"OK! We'll set up shop here to the right of the entrance."

Brian ran in. Fifteen minutes later, he returned with a clean face, some bags of chips, bottles of water, and a bowl for Gaby. He emptied a water bottle into the bowl, and Gaby eagerly lapped it up in record time. I poured water over his eyes, trying to wash away the gunk caked in a circle around his eyelids.

"He keeps pawing at his eyes, Brian. I sure wish I could wash this yellow stuff off him—look at him. Completely caked in it." Our yellow bodies were a constant reminder of the hell we had been through.

I left Gaby with Brian and went inside. I was surprised that the greeter who had so kindly let us in didn't seem shocked by my appearance. I guess he'd gotten used to the sight. I headed toward the restrooms at the back of the store, passing televisions, camcorders, video games, and the in-store café. I could smell pizza and hot dogs, which reminded me how hungry I was.

As I walked by, the people in the café froze. No one spoke or even chewed. They just stared at me. All of them. No one said a word. Worse, not one of them gave me a sympathetic look or even a quizzical expression. No one asked what had happened to me or why I was wearing a nightgown or how I how I got covered in yellow dust. I'm normally a thick-skinned person, but the stares from these couple of dozen people unnerved me.

I couldn't tell what was offending these diners the most. My nightgown? My lack of a bra? I wouldn't normally be caught dead in public without a bra, yet now here I was, in a thin nightgown that showed everything. I wanted to scream at these people: "What are you staring at? Do you think I like being in this condition?" But I just kept walking and pretended I didn't notice their stares.

I realize now I was assuming the worst about these people, who were almost certainly not judging my appearance but just had no idea what to do or say. I'm sure they had heard about the attacks, but coming face to face with someone who had obviously lived through the destruction must have made the danger feel uncomfortably close. Whatever they were thinking or feeling, I desperately needed a hug or smile or some sign of sympathy.

When I finally reached the bathroom, I was frustrated to find a queue of women stretching outside the door. The line was a mix of yellow-tinged people and bewildered BJ's shoppers. My eyes were really hurting now, so I slipped into the bathroom to get to the empty sinks. I turned on the tap and started looking for a way to wash my eyes. I tried sticking my eye directly into the water stream. I collected water into my cupped hands and blinked my eye rapidly while submerging it. When I could feel some relief, I cautiously blotted my eyes dry.

I left the bathroom and wandered around the store until I found a cheap bra and basic black flip-flops. I purchased them with $15 of Brian's cash, and then went back to the bathroom to change. I relished the triumphal moment when I took off those filthy socks and threw them in the bathroom wastebasket. I was so focused on getting a bra and some shoes that I didn't even think about buying anything else to wear!

I put my dirty nightgown back on and walked toward the front of the store, where a row of TVs were all airing coverage of the day's horrific news. I was astonished when a TV station flashed the current time: 3:00 p.m.

I can't believe it. It's 3:00 p.m., and I'm just starting to learn the full scope of the news. People around the world have been watching their TVs to get the latest updates, but I've been walking around in the middle of it, and I barely know anything.

Who did this? Why? What was the extent of the destruction? How many were killed? How was our government responding? Six hours after the first attack, I learned for the first time that there had been four hijacked planes: two hit the World Trade Center towers, one hit the Pentagon, and one crashed in a field in Pennsylvania after its passengers charged the cockpit and diverted the hijackers.

The news was awful, but at least Brian and I finally knew that the attacks had not been as widespread as the rumors we had heard that morning. Safely out of Manhattan, and feeling semi-humanized after visiting the bathroom and getting a bra and shoes, I felt a sense of hope for the first time that day.

6

A Car, a Room, and
New Obstacles

INITIALLY, BRIAN AND I TOOK TURNS watching the TVs inside the store while the other sat with Gaby outside. But we didn't like being apart, so Brian bought a small battery-run boom box so we could sit outside together and listen to the news. Though we no longer seemed to be in danger, we were still in unfamiliar territory and had no way of communicating if we got separated.

I wanted to call our families, but the line at the phone booth remained prohibitively long. "Brian, I see some people using their cell phones. Maybe service is back up?"

"Maybe. Let's try to borrow someone's cell," Brian said.

Scanning the crowd, I noticed a BJ's shopper who seemed very intrigued by those of us hanging out in the front of the building. I marched up to her and asked, "Ma'am, is your cell phone working? I know this is a big request, but do you mind if I borrow your phone for five minutes? We were evacuated out of Manhattan, and I'm sure my mom in Florida is worried about me."

Lord, I pray that sounded genuine and not melodramatic. I pray I've approached a sympathetic person!

To my relief, she answered, "Yes, sure, of course!"

Thank you, Lord!

I called my mom and was amazed that the call went through.

"Hi, Mom, it's me. We're OK. We have Gaby with us and he's OK. We're in New Jersey; I'll call you back later." I raced through a monologue, barely giving my mom a chance to respond. I didn't want to initiate a long conversation on a borrowed phone—and I wasn't ready to tell my mother any details of our day. I handed the phone to Brian, and he spoke to his mother in the same speedy style.

"Thank you so much, I can't thank you enough," I said as I returned the cell phone, hoping this woman knew what a gift she'd given us. Both our moms now knew we were OK and safe. I thought about all the people who still didn't know what had happened to their loved ones. I had been with my husband all day, communicating face to face with the person dearest to me. It must have been awful to be alone in the midst of a terrible tragedy.

Returning to our spot on the ground, we continued monitoring the news—learning for the first time what most of the country had known for hours.

+ Streets were sealed off below 14th Street.
+ Orders had been given to evacuate everyone below Canal Street.
+ All flights had been grounded across the country; no commercial flights were being allowed in U.S. airspace.
+ The entire airline industry had officially shut down.
+ Fighter jets were patrolling the skies over New York.
+ New York City Mayor Rudy Giuliani had ordered all Manhattan borders to be sealed off; all bridges and tunnels were closed to protect public safety. No New York City mayor had ever ordered this done before.

"Brian, I can't believe all the planes in the US have been grounded. I didn't even know that was possible."

"Our neighborhood must be a ghost town now," Brian said. "Mayor Giuliani said 'forced evacuations.' Do you think anyone voluntarily stayed?"

The list of closings and evacuations seemed endless: the Metropolitan Museum and the Empire State building were closed. Major League Baseball games and college classes were canceled. Disney World had shut down. The Mall of America in Minneapolis was cleared. Hoover Dam and Mount Rushmore were closed.

I noticed other evacuees leaning over to listen in. A middle-aged couple asked, "Do you mind if we join you?"

"Absolutely not. Feel free to sit with us," Brian said. Others quickly followed. We began discussing the morning's events, comparing notes of where we had been and how we had escaped, and sharing our opinions of what should happen next.

At one point, a newscaster announced, "Osama bin Laden, one of the founders of Al-Qaeda, is suspected in having instigated the attacks." I'd never heard of Osama bin Laden. I pay attention to the news in my daily life, but I was totally blindsided by this unfamiliar name.

"I had no idea anyone out there hated us enough to do something like this!" Most of the people around me nodded, and I was relieved to know I hadn't been living with my head in the sand the past few years.

By now it was late afternoon, and Brian and I were becoming concerned about where we would spend the night. Our "Boombox BJ's Group," as I had started to call us, began discussing rumors we had heard about available accommodations.

"All the hotels in New Jersey anywhere near Manhattan are booked!"

"There are no rental cars left around here."

Every rumor heightened my anxiety. Would we have to sleep in this parking lot in front of the BJ's? Compared to what we had been through it didn't sound that terrible, and looking at the number of evacuees around us, it looked like we wouldn't be alone. But I so wanted to get a shower and lie on a soft bed.

About 5:30, a young guy who had just joined our group said, "I've heard a nearby Dollar Rent-a-Car still has cars available. Me and my friend are going to walk over and see. Want to go check it out with us?"

It seemed too good to be true, but Brian was cautiously

hopeful. "Sure, it's definitely worth the effort!" We said good-bye to the rest of the group and headed across the parking lot toward the Newport Mall, where we discovered a parking garage that included several car rental companies.

I felt like we had won the lottery when we found out Dollar Rent-a-Car had cars available.

Brian began to fill out the paperwork, but as he signed the con-tract, the sales associate told him, "We only have our higher-end models left, and we have a three-day policy minimum. You can't rent it for just one day."

"I've never heard of such a policy," Brian said, suspiciously. "I'm sure you're aware of the situation many of us have found ourselves in. And isn't this a much higher rate than normal?"

The sales associate coldly told us, "It's up to you."

I pulled my husband a few feet away.

"Brian," I reasoned in a low voice, "the borders into Manhattan might remain closed for a while, so we will probably make that minimum anyway. I'm just happy to have a car. Can we just sign the contract and go?"

Thoughts of a hotel room where we could shower, eat a meal, lie down, and have some peace were making me eager to get on the road as soon as possible, no matter what the cost or terms. Brian signed the contract.

We drove through New Jersey for nearly an hour before attempting to find a hotel. Having Gaby with us made the search harder, since many hotels didn't allow dogs. We struck out at sev-eral places before stopping at an expensive chain in Parsippany, about twenty miles west of Manhattan. Brian parked, and we all three went in, determined to get a room this time.

We were the only ones in the lobby, which featured a mar-ble floor, Queen Anne-style furniture, and tall palm trees. The receptionist at the check-in desk looked us up and down. We were beyond filthy, probably quite smelly, and utterly exhausted.

"I'm sorry, we don't take pets."

I looked at Brian, who was turning beet red.

"Can I speak to the hotel manager, please?" Brian demanded.

"One moment," she said passively, picking up the phone. After ten minutes, an older gentleman came to the front desk. Brian turned on his business presentation voice and explained the events of the day and why we needed a hotel room so badly, even offering to purchase a higher-priced room "if it helped."

As I listened, I got angrier and angrier that we were being reduced to begging in order to get a frickin' hotel room.

"OK, we can accept the situation for one night, but one night only," the manager finally said blandly. Brian handed over his credit card. Even though they had just heard our whole story, neither the manager nor the receptionist offered any hint of sympathy or the slightest gesture of helpfulness. It was clear they simply wanted us to leave the lobby as soon as possible.

As Brian took the room key, I noticed a sign on the counter: "FORGOT SOMETHING? WE HAVE COMPLIMENTARY TOILETRIES!" I asked the receptionist, "Can I have some toiletries, please?"

"Which ones?"

I almost laughed. She'd heard our story, saw that we carried no luggage, purse, or backpack—not even a plastic bag. We stood in front of her like wax museum exhibits, red-eyed and completely yellow except for our washed faces. I was in my short nightgown. My thin, short hair had been dust-styled into coarse clumps that were sticking out in all directions.

I managed to say through gritted teeth, "All, please." She gave me a handful of items. I scurried to the elevator, shocked by the lack of compassion.

As soon as we opened the door, I scooped up Gaby and dashed directly to the tub. I repositioned the showerhead to spray a strong stream on Gaby's coat, trying to wash all the gunk away before I lathered him up. It looked like I had thrown a large bowl of oatmeal into the tub. I rubbed and scrubbed his fur for a full fifteen minutes before the water began running clear. Then I climbed into the shower with him, and it was another fifteen minutes before the water was running clear again.

Normally Gaby liked to be washed, and he would shake, snort, and "fake sneeze" to show he was enjoying himself. But tonight he stood completely still with his head down. I felt so bad about what he had been through, and we couldn't even explain it to him. While drying him off with a towel, I noticed how red his eyes were. He kept rubbing them with his paws.

I wrapped myself in the large hotel towel and sat down on the bed. We called our moms from our hotel room phone, eager to talk to them longer.

"I'd been playing tennis during the attacks," Mom said. "One of the employees of the country club came down to the courts to tell all of us players the news. I drove home quickly, and walked in to about thirty messages from friends and family who were worried about you. For the rest of the day, I waited by the phone, hoping you would call."

I gave her a quick rundown of our day, and she started crying. "I'm so glad you and Brian are OK!"

She then began asking questions. "So where will you go now? What are you going to do? Why don't you just drive down to Tallahassee since you have a car?"

I considered her idea for a half-second. After the day we had just endured, Tallahassee sounded like utopia!

But I pushed the idea aside. "We can't just leave, Mom. We have to go back."

"Go back to what? From what the news says, New York City

is still under siege, and you don't even have a home to return to!"

"Mom," I reasoned, "I don't consider my apartment my home. The City is my home. I have to return. We've got to get back into the City. We've got to go back home."

I had to practically hold the phone away from my ear as my mother squawked her outrage. She had never understood my love for New York.

Brian's mom had heard the news on the radio at work. "I knew Brian was supposed to interview for jobs this week, and I was worried that he might have been in one of the towers!"

After reassuring our moms, I called Sarah, a Manhattan friend I had known for years. "I assume our place won't be open for a while, Sarah, if it survived at all. Can we stay with you until we figure out what to do next?"

She yelled, "Of course! I'm just so glad you guys are OK! I've been worried about you all day."

I asked if she had heard from other mutual friends. Because most of my friends were transplants to New York with no family close by, we had become like family to each other as we tried to make our way into acting and dancing roles. This group of friends-turned-family was the real reason I didn't want to head to Tallahassee tomorrow—I felt the need to return to the City to process this trauma with them.

***

We ordered room service, including a hamburger patty for Gaby. He sniffed it, took a few bites, and then threw up the little bit he had eaten. We had never seen him do that before.

At 8:30 we sat down to watch President George W. Bush speak to the nation.

> Tonight, I ask for your prayers for all those who grieve, for the children whose worlds have been shattered, for all whose sense of safety and security has been threatened. And I pray they will be

comforted by a Power greater than any of us, spoken through the ages in Psalm 23: *Even though I walk through the valley of the shadow of death, I fear no evil, for you are with me.*

"I love it that he mentioned the Bible," Brian said, "and especially that verse. If there was *ever* a time to do it, *now* is the time for our nation to acknowledge God and our need for him...." He stopped, choked up.

After the presidential address, we saw clips of New York Mayor Rudy Giuliani that had been filmed earlier in the day.

"I'm declaring a state of emergency. The present conditions imperil public safety. I urge New Yorkers to stay home Wednesday if they can. . . . The number of casualties will be more than any of us can bear ultimately. I don't think we want to speculate on the number of casualties. The effort now has to be to save as many people as possible."

Although no one wanted to speculate, I had heard that as many as 10,000 people might have died in the Twin Towers. I agonized over that number. I was also horrified to find out that so many firefighters and police officers were missing. When we had been running away from the burning towers, we saw scores of fire trucks and ambulances racing toward them. How many of those first responders that rushed past us had been killed when the buildings collapsed?

"Brian, they've hardly found anyone alive."

"Maybe they'll find more—the rescue has really just started." Brian tried to reassure me, but he wasn't terribly convincing. "It must be hard to get to them. I mean, fires are still raging, and more buildings are collapsing."

"Could our building collapse?"

"It's definitely a possibility," Brian said sadly.

We kept switching between news coverage, looking for video footage of the Financial District, hoping we might catch a glimpse of our apartment building. We could see that a strong wind had blown smoke from the fires southward all day long.

My heart began pounding suddenly as I thought about our apartment. Brian and I looked at each other. "We didn't close the terrace doors!" we said at practically the same time.

"Our apartment must be seriously damaged, Christina." Brian seemed uncharacteristically anxious.

"Dammit! I can't believe I rushed out the door and forgot everything. I'm so sorry, Brian!"

Even though the news was horrific, we couldn't bring ourselves to turn it off, so we left the TV on all night. Although exhausted, we hardly slept at all.

7

An Unrecognizable City:
Wednesday, September 12

WE AWAKENED TO SOME ENCOURAGING NEWS. "The PATH train is running on a modified schedule," a newscaster stated.

"Brian, oh my gosh, did you hear that? The PATH is open!"

The Port Authority Trans-Hudson (PATH) train goes underneath the Hudson River, linking Manhattan to New Jersey. Manhattan was not completely shut down to the outside world today. Although we knew we couldn't get into our neighborhood, the chance to return to Manhattan was a big step toward going home! And it meant we could get to Sarah's apartment.

Groggy after a near-sleepless night and still wrapped in my towel, I was suddenly jolted awake by a horrifying realization.

"Brian, I don't have any clothes! Did you get any yesterday at BJ's? I have nothing to wear other than my awful yellow-covered nightgown!"

Brian shook his head glumly. "I didn't think about it either."

"I cannot believe I didn't think about buying an outfit while at BJ's! What a bonehead: to have settled for just a bra and flip-flops."

Even while I chastised myself, however, I became very aware of why I hadn't thought to buy clothes. I slowly started to put my thoughts into words.

"I just didn't consider the idea because, well, because I just wasn't in my right mind. I was so bent on getting a bra and shoes and so relieved when I put them on. Maybe that sent a signal to my brain that I was OK? Plus, I was *so filthy*. I was focused on getting a shower and didn't think for a second what I would need after that!"

I tried to stop beating myself up about my irrational behavior from the day before and started looking for a solution. "I didn't see a shop in the lobby," I said, flipping through the hotel's amenities folder. "Could we somehow get clothes to the hotel?" It was 9:00. What would even be open? "I would do anything to avoid putting that gross thing on again. I can't believe I wore it all day yesterday."

Eventually, I realized that I would have to either leave the hotel naked or put on the gown, which I could smell from two feet away—a combination of smoke and some kind of soured, putrid stench. It was completely caked with the yellow dust, which had not been shaken loose through all our wanderings the day before. I put it over my head and immediately felt a million little splinters attacking my skin. I looked at myself in the mirror.

This thing isn't fit to be used as a rag to clean a car. In fact, it would probably scratch up a car! No wonder people were staring at me at the BJ's.

"All right, let's get outta here," I said, as I leashed Gaby. "Let's get something to eat, get some clothes, and get back home!"

I tried to hold my head high despite my disgusting clothes as we left the hotel. We hit the drive-through of a fast-food chain for breakfast and headed back toward the rental car depot. I tried to feed Gaby, who refused to eat. As we neared Newport, we saw a strip mall that included some cheap clothing stores.

Brian parked the car and said, "You go first this time. Here, take a credit card." I walked into the store, which had just opened for the day, and immediately felt the stares from the two employees.

Embarrassed and frustrated, I grabbed a shirt and pants and put them on in the dressing room in record time. Both were ill-fitting, unflattering, and poorly made, but I didn't care. I was so happy to have something clean on my body. I paid for the clothes, ran outside, and slam-dunked my disgusting gown into the garbage.

I waited in the car with Gaby while Brian headed into the men's store. He soon came out wearing a new shirt and shorts, and we headed back to the rental car drop-off. "We'll just be charging you for the one day, not three," the sales associate sweetly told us. As we were walking to the Newport PATH station, Brian commented, "Maybe word got around about the price-gouging, and the car rental companies received backlash."

I shrugged my shoulders, relieved things worked out, but not really caring why. I was focused on returning to Manhattan.

I had taken a PATH train multiple times from the World Trade Center to Newark, but the World Trade Center terminal had been destroyed the day before, so we had to take the train to 33rd Street in Manhattan.

"Brian, I've never ridden this train before. And I'm scared. I don't want to travel under water through a tunnel—what if it's a target?"

I started thinking about where the train would wind up in Manhattan: Herald Square, near Manhattan landmarks like Macy's and the Empire State Building and Penn Station. What if the terrorists were gunning for those spots today? I wanted to avoid tall buildings and famous sites right now. I was afraid to ride the train, and I was afraid to get off the train.

"We're just going to have to do it. You can shut your eyes if you need to," Brian consoled.

"Shut? I need both of them open in case we have to run!" We boarded the train and sat down—the only ones in our car.

"Geez, this feels so eerie. It's 11:30 a.m. The train should be packed," I said. When you live in a crowded city, there is nothing more unnerving than being alone.

During the fifteen-minute ride, I quelled my fears by concentrating on my love of the City and my determination to return to it. We arrived at the 33rd Street station and walked up the stairs into Greeley Square.

"Brian, have we gotten off at the wrong stop?"

I turned back to double-check the station's signage. We had ascended into one of Manhattan's densest areas, where hundreds of people clog the sidewalks day and night and drivers honk impatiently in gridlocked traffic. Today, we heard no horns and saw almost no cars or pedestrians. A caustic, sulfuric odor filled my nostrils as soon as we reached street level.

"Gee," I whispered to Brian, lowering my voice self-consciously. "Mayor Giuliani urged people to stay home from work today, and it appears almost everyone obeyed!"

A group of fighter jets streaked overhead. The few people in the streets collectively looked up, nervous and on high alert.

Man, look at all of us. We're so scared about planes now. We should feel relieved we're being protected, but our first instinct is to run for cover.

The City was hauntingly quiet, as if intense sorrow had thrown a blanket over everyone and everything. In a matter of minutes, Brian and I had gone from a pristine New Jersey town where it was just another Wednesday to a shocked city paralyzed in grief and fear.

We headed for Sarah's apartment, passing only a few people as we walked. No one was rushing. No one wore a suit, but most were wearing face masks over their nose and mouth.

"Christina, look at all the flyers!" Brian said.

Paper flyers were attached to every available surface. Light posts. Shop windows. Traffic lights. Mailboxes. On every flyer was a picture of at least one person, smiling or serious, looking out from professional photos and family snapshots. These were the missing; most of them had been workers in or near the World Trade Center. The flyers were pleas from their loved ones who were looking for information.

The area was fluttering with copy paper, and people were buzzing from flyer to flyer like bees in a flower garden. The volume was overwhelming and devastating.

Leaflets had also been tacked up with information for people like us, who had lived Downtown and were now homeless. Several schools were ready to accommodate those who needed a bed, and some locations were parceling out donated food and clothing. I took mental notes and grabbed copies of these notices when I could, relieved to know help was available.

Few stores were open, but we spotted people streaming out of a nearby bodega, juggling grocery bags and large jugs of water.

"Brian, let's stop to get a few things. Especially face masks," I urged.

I grabbed two face masks from the bodega, but there seemed to be little else left on its bare shelves. I snapped up a large bottle of lukewarm water and bought a *New York Post*, which I had read almost every day in the eight years I had lived in New York. Somehow I felt surprised to see a September 12 edition; I assumed newsrooms and distribution would be at a standstill. The headline screamed: *Act of War, World Trade Center Destroyed; Many Dead*. A picture of the plane ramming into the South Tower filled the rest of the cover.

Continuing on to Sarah's, we noticed people were lined up three to four deep, waiting to use pay phones, which seemed odd since nearly everyone had cell phones these days.

Lots of the people we saw were crying. Some were crying in groups, others were crying alone. Instead of fighting over cabs and pushing through the crowds, New Yorkers—strangers—were comforting each other. I'd never seen anything like it—I didn't even know that New Yorkers were capable of such compassion.

Clusters of candles crackled underneath flyers, near the entrances of buildings, on windowsills. U.S. flags swung from street signs, waved from shop entrances, and hung from apartment balconies.

"It's like the City has exploded into American patriotism," Brian said. Just then, a fire truck passed. People ran to the edge of the sidewalk and whooped and hollered and waved flags. After yesterday, people had a completely new appreciation for firefighters.

"Wow! It's like a giant American pep rally!" I stammered, surprised by the spontaneous display of sentiment. When I saw a guy hawking flags, I asked, "Brian, do we have a few dollars for a flag?"

"Sure," Brian responded, giving me his wallet. I selected a small flag and an American flag scarf that I tied as a bandana around Gaby's collar.

The walk up 9th Avenue through Hell's Kitchen stretched longer and longer as we stopped to read the flyers and gawk at the alien sights and sounds all around us. By the time we rang the buzzer at Sarah's 46th Street building, we had spent almost two hours—when the walk would have normally taken thirty minutes—in this bewildering environment, crossing thirteen blocks and three avenues and witnessing one massive funeral. I felt close to tears when Sarah's voice crackled on the intercom. "Hello, who is this?"

"It's us! We made it!"

8

Looking for Order in the Chaos

WHEN SARAH BUZZED US IN, we stepped into the lobby with feelings of triumph and relief, as if crossing the finish line of a bizarre marathon.

Sarah and Jeff came flying down the stairs to meet us.

"Boy are we glad to see you!" I said as we all hugged.

"Ditto, girl. We were worried sick," Sarah replied, as we climbed the stairs to her third-floor apartment.

"How did you wind up here?" I asked Jeff. I liked Jeff a lot, who had been dating my friend for over a year, but I wasn't expecting him to be here; he lives in Brooklyn.

"I was working at the Wall Street office yesterday, and we evacuated our building after the second tower was hit. I was a few blocks away when the first tower collapsed. Everyone around me headed over the Brooklyn Bridge to get away from Manhattan, but I just wanted to be with Sarah. I walked the six miles to her apartment since the subways were shut down.

"It took me forever to get here," Jeff said, "because I kept stopping to turn around and look at the towers and to talk with everyone around me. Can you imagine? New Yorkers talking to strangers on the street? I saw the strangest things—like construction workers hosing soot off people passing by!"

Sarah said, "I was so relieved when he finally showed up at my door."

"Are you sure you don't mind us staying?" Sarah had a very small apartment, and I didn't want to be a burden, especially since

Jeff was here too. But being together was comforting.

"Of course not! My roommate's away and you can stay in her room, if you don't mind bunk beds."

Later, Sarah and I walked to a nearby Italian restaurant where she waitressed. But when I tried to order a glass of wine, I ran into an unexpected problem.

"Can I see your ID?" the waiter asked.

I felt my cheeks get hot. "I don't have my ID," I stammered.

"I'm sorry, but I can't serve you alcohol unless you have your ID," the waiter responded icily.

"I'll handle this, Christina," Sarah said, asking to see the manager. "Listen, my friend here had to escape her Financial District apartment in her pajamas and nothing else. She and her husband are staying with me now. She wants a glass of wine."

"Of course we'll bring you one," the manager responded, giving the waiter a pointed look.

"Thanks, Sarah. It hadn't occurred to me that I couldn't even buy a glass of wine without my ID. This is going to be a lot harder than I realized!"

Back at Sarah's apartment, I sat on the floor and tried to feed Gaby. As soon as he took a bite, he threw it up. I scrubbed Sarah's rug while Brian and I looked at each other with worry.

We spent the rest of the evening watching the news, hungry for any information. We learned how nineteen men from Saudi Arabia, the United Arab Emirates, Egypt, and Lebanon had carefully planned the attacks for months, even attending flight schools in my home state of Florida to learn to fly the jets. We discovered that they had probably carried simple but lethal tools like pocket knives and box cutters onto the planes—tools that could legally be carried onto flights—and that they had entered four planes scheduled for cross-country trips, which meant they were carrying full loads of jet fuel. The hijackers had then overpowered the flight crews and turned the passenger jets into flying missiles.

I was especially intrigued by reports about the speed of the planes. One newscaster reported that the plane was flying about 590 miles per hour when it struck the South Tower; planes are normally flying above 10,000 feet when they achieve that speed.

"No wonder our ears hurt so badly afterward," I said.

"Wow," Brian said. "We were barely 500 feet below that plane while we stood on the terrace!"

I searched for our building any time I saw news footage from Lower Manhattan. I never saw the building itself, but I could tell that thick smoke from the fires was still blowing straight south toward our building and our lovely terrace—the feature we had been most excited about when we chose the apartment before returning to New York. But we had run away and left the terrace doors wide open, never imagining it would be putting our home in jeopardy.

On Thursday morning, after a fitful night's sleep on Sarah's roommate's bunk bed, Brian and I grew even more concerned about Gaby, who was completely lethargic and had no interest in food. We took him to a vet near Sarah's apartment and explained what Gaby had been through in the past few days.

"This is the only dog I've seen who experienced the attacks first-hand like he did," the vet told us. "He's been through a lot, so I'll make sure we look at everything. Leave him here overnight so we can observe him."

Brian and I tried to be brave for each other, but we both were upset at having to leave Gaby. On our way back to the apartment, I told Brian I wanted to go on alone to look for some new clothes and check on our mail. I wanted to be by myself, and I was hoping that walking would help me expend some of my nervous energy.

We had learned that mail for Lower Manhattan neighborhoods was being disbursed from the James A. Farley building, an eight-acre building near Madison Square Garden that spans

the width of two city blocks. It took me less than twenty minutes to reach the building, but the wait in line took more than an
hour. From what I could tell, only two employees were dispensing
mail to the scores of Lower Manhattan residents who were there.
After all that time, I was handed only two pieces of junk mail.
We usually received about ten to fifteen bills and letters per day.

I wondered what had happened to all the mail that had been
in transit on Tuesday—did delivery trucks burn in the fires or get
destroyed when the towers tumbled? And now all flights across
the country had been grounded, so no mail was moving by air.
"I'll never take small things like mail for granted again," I vowed.

The lack of mail service made me even more grateful for the
emails that I discovered when I logged into Sarah's computer
later that day. "Wow! High school friends, college friends, fellow actors—even acquaintances have left sweet messages for me,"
I told Brian.

"Christina, HOW ARE YOU???????? I haven't heard from you,
and I've contacted others who told me they hadn't heard from you
either," read the message from Cindy, a dear friend from high
school. "PLEASE tell us you're all right! Everyone is so worried
about you and Brian! We love you!"

"Boy, I really feel so loved right now. It's awesome," I said, writ-
ing back to Cindy to tell her we were OK.

I blamed still-spotty phone service for not trying harder to
connect with faraway friends and family. In reality, I felt too pre-
occupied with just getting through each moment of each day to
spend a lot of time communicating.

The attacks on the World Trade Center were considered a
criminal act, so all of Lower Manhattan was being treated like a
massive crime scene, even while the search for survivors continued. It was like the lower section of the island had been cordoned
off by one very long strip of yellow crime scene tape, and no one
was being allowed to return to their homes or businesses. The

area was now being described as the "Frozen Zone," while the blocks surrounding the fallen towers were being described as "Ground Zero."

Desperate for news, Brian called our landlord on Thursday afternoon. "Do you have any information on our building? Has it suffered any damage? When can we expect to get back?"

The landlord responded to all questions by saying, "We're not sure."

So I was ecstatic to find a small notice in the *New York Post* that said Lower Manhattan residents would be able to return briefly with National Guard escorts to collect belongings; people with abandoned pets or needing medications were being given priority.

"All we have to do is show up at Pier 40," I said. "If I had just a few minutes at home to grab some things, I know I could breathe easier. I left my wedding ring, my purse, and other valuables out in plain view. They would all be easy targets for looters if they get into our building. And my wallet and ID are in my purse!"

Financial loss was certainly a concern, but it also masked my deeper longing—I just wanted to go home. Sarah and Jeff offered to go with us, so we made plans to set out early the next morning.

9

The Frozen Zone:
Friday, September 14

I WENT TO BED EARLY, planning to rest up for the journey to our apartment, but I slept very little. When I finally dozed off, I dreamed I was alone in a huge field of waist-high yellow grass. I was standing with my head tilted back and my mouth wide open, screaming bloody murder to the sky. But there was no one to hear me—I was completely alone in an endless field, just screaming and screaming. I woke with a start and never fell back to sleep.

Apparently no one else slept well either because all four of us were up by 6:00, and after watching the news were out the door by 9:00 a.m. We were headed toward the Number One subway line that would transport us to Pier 40. More people were on the streets today than when we had returned two days ago, but the City was still eerily quiet for a Friday. Fears about Gaby hung over me like a dark cloud, but the weather was beautiful, and I was excited by the prospect of returning to the apartment, even if it was just for a few minutes.

As we approached the Pier 40 terminal, I noticed pet crates stacked outside the building and police cars waiting on the highway. People were streaming toward the old pier from all directions. "I never expected to see this many people! There was only a tiny mention of this in the *Post.*"

We entered through glass double doors into a cavernous room—and complete chaos. Hundreds of people were already there—standing in groups, sitting on the floor, milling about aimlessly. Some were talking; many were shouting. No one seemed to be in charge, and there was no sign that anyone was being transported anywhere. My excitement quickly faded and my anxiety rose.

Two men in front of us erupted into a shouting match. "I should get to go Downtown before you! My dog is more important than your computer!"

I turned to a woman standing quietly nearby. "What's going on? Do you know?"

"They started escorting people an hour ago, right when I arrived," she responded, "but it hasn't made a dent. There simply isn't enough transportation for everyone here. So they just announced that they weren't letting anyone in unless they needed to rescue a pet."

She continued, "Those that weren't here for pets were told to leave. Many left, but others refused. They are still arguing to be taken downtown to retrieve things they want."

Turning to our group, I whispered, "Look at all these people. They're just like us. We all evacuated with only the clothes on our backs, and everyone is desperate to get back home."

"They're desperate all right," Jeff said. "A bunch of them look like they're ready to start hitting someone! This might be pent-up emotions people have been carrying around since Tuesday. Maybe it's just coming out now."

As we stood just inside the door, stunned by the chaos, I noticed that Sarah was crying. In the seven years I'd known Sarah, I had seen her cry only once. Her calm, cool, and collected temperament had always served to moderate my passionate and emotional personality. Today, I was actually somewhat reassured by her display of emotion.

OK, if Sarah's crying, then I know I'm not overreacting. This is bad. Oh Lord, please heal these people here. I know you care about them, and everyone is in such pain!

"Dang it! My hopes had been so high that we would get to

go back," I said. But I felt selfish for being so frustrated when I thought about the thousands of pets that had to be stranded all over Lower Manhattan.

"What if we hadn't been home that morning?" I wondered out loud. "Gaby would still be there all alone. He wouldn't have had any water or food. He would've been so scared. He might have been killed by the smoke or fire, especially with the doors open over the last four days."

"Yes, at least he was with us that day," Brian said somberly. "At least we were able to get him out and to the vet. I hope he's doing OK today, poor guy."

The woman who had told us about the transport turned back to me. "You know some of the people who are here today are trying to retrieve pets from apartments of people they know died in the attacks."

"No way!" I was shocked at the altruism, and my change in attitude was complete. I now wanted these people to get into the area even more than I wanted to go close my terrace doors.

A few minutes later, Brian pulled the four of us together. "You guys, there's no way we'll be able to get to our apartment today from here. Let's leave and try to get down to the Frozen Zone on our own. I'd rather do that than stay here any longer. I can't take this scene."

We nodded, and he led us out of the terminal. "Let's get ourselves to Canal Street and see if we can breach the barricade there and walk the rest of the way."

I was incredulous. "We can't get past Canal Street. It's all over the news. They're not letting a fly down there. Why the heck do you think they'll let us schmucks in? What do we tell them when we get down there? 'Officer, we just have to get past so we can shut some doors in our apartment'? Shoot, they'll laugh at us!"

I looked at Sarah and Jeff, expecting them to agree with me. Instead, Jeff said, "Let's try it. What have we got to lose?" Sarah nodded in solidarity.

"Fine, but I'm not getting arrested for this. However, I will come bail you all out of jail after you get locked up," I said, only half-joking.

We walked the few blocks from Houston to Canal Street. Even though I knew the area had been blocked off, the eerie stillness on Canal shocked me. There was no traffic and only a few people on the sidewalks. Normally, you could catch a glimpse from here all the way down to the World Trade Center complex, but today all we could see was smoke. Fire trucks, police vans, and construction equipment were everywhere. It felt like we were on the cusp of hell.

Although we were only a few blocks from our apartment, Brian plotted a roundabout route in an attempt to maximize our chance of getting into the area. Walking east on Canal, we passed from Tribeca into the heart of Chinatown, which was quiet and almost deserted. Police barriers were posted along the south side of the street, with cops positioned every few blocks.

At Bowery Street, Brian stopped. "OK, let's try it here," he said, motioning toward a police officer standing at the corner of Bowery and Canal. "I'll take the lead on this."

I was glad Brian wanted to do the talking because I didn't think the policeman would let us past, and I didn't want to be yelled at. I had reached my daily quota of anger and drama. As the three of us trailed behind, Brian headed straight to the officer, who was facing us from behind the barrier.

"Hi, Officer," he began, calmly, respectfully. "We live Downtown, and we need to get back into our apartment. We have to do a few things to secure our place—we're worried about looters. Can we get by?"

"No, no one can get by," the officer responded. "No one can go south of Canal Street. Sorry." He was firm but not mean. Brian thanked him, turned to the three of us, and indicated we should keep walking east. I knew he intended to try again. A few blocks later, at Forsyth Street, Brian tried again. He walked up to an officer and offered the same spiel, adding, "We don't plan to stay at our place more than half an hour."

The officer looked us all up and down. "Identification, please."

Brian pulled out his wallet and showed the officer his driver's license. The officer looked it over, looked at me, and asked, "Identification, please." I felt intimidated, tongue-tied, and instantly frustrated.

"My wife evacuated without getting her driver's license. She doesn't have it," Brian told him. The officer silently looked at me for what seemed like two minutes. Finally, he said, "OK, go on. Do these two also live Downtown?"

"No, we don't," Jeff said.

Brian added, "They're our friends who are here just to help us out."

"Well, they can't go," the officer responded simply. "Only you two. And keep your ID out. You'll probably be asked again by another officer."

"Sarah and Jeff, we'll catch you later at your place," Brian said. They turned to return to the subway, and we walked around the barrier, thanking the officer profusely.

Brian and I looked at each other with relief, though we felt too nervous to talk. I couldn't believe it had worked.

Brian's my hero. And I'm SOOO glad he grabbed his wallet.

We walked directly south for half a mile, until we passed Wall Street, and then snaked our way west down the haphazard alleys in the heart of the historic Financial District. We walked fast, hugging the buildings in an effort to be as inconspicuous as possible.

I had walked these streets hundreds of times, but today it was like walking through a foreign city—a gray, dust-covered ghost town. It's what I imagined Chernobyl would look like. What I imagined the end of the world would look like.

All the stores were closed. Buildings were dark. There was no electricity. The sulfuric stench of burning electrical wires was almost thick enough to taste—as prominent as it had been when the towers first fell. Papers, dirt, and chunks of concrete were piled haphazardly on top of yellow-coated cars, awnings, and trash cans. Scraps of twisted metal hung from windowsills and fire escapes. The farther we walked, the more rattled I became. I kept my head down, looking only at my feet, to avoid seeing the destruction.

About forty minutes after we had crossed the barricade, we finally reached Broadway, near the bull sculpture. Trying to avoid being noticed, we took a few extra minutes to cut through the short alley connecting Broadway and Greenwich Street. I was happily surprised that no other officer had approached us. Now all we had to do was cross a narrow pedestrian bridge that passes over the Brooklyn Battery Tunnel and connects Greenwich and Washington Streets.

Instead of a short pedestrian bridge, we found a daunting hurdle filled with debris. We "waded" our way over the congested bridge as if we were wading through a muddy, weedy creek, kicking aside knee-high debris composed of concrete, papers, scraps of metal, and general trash. We finally made it across and stepped up to the front of our building. I looked up and realized we had beaten the odds, fighting our way back to the spot we had fled in terror just four days earlier.

10

A Surreal Zombie Apartment

I LOOKED UP AT LE RIVAGE, the building I had been so proud to call home. Typically a golden color, the building was now a dull, mustard yellow, coated in dust so thick that I could barely tell the difference between windows and the brick facade.

Afternoon sunlight illuminated dusty disarray inside the lobby. Flo, the building's concierge, wasn't behind the desk, but Gus, a maintenance worker, ran over as soon as we walked in.

"Brian and Christina! How have you two been?"

"We've been all over the place, Gus," Brian answered, giving him a hug. "How the heck are you? Where's Flo?"

"Flo stayed in the building for a few days, but she was finally able to go home to her family in Staten Island yesterday," Gus explained. "Three of us have been here around the clock, sleeping in the lobby to keep out anybody who shouldn't be here. We plan to stay to keep watch over everything."

Gus seemed thrilled to talk to us, as if he hadn't had a conversation for days. He told us all about what had happened after we ran away. "People ran in from the street for shelter when the towers came down. Later, firefighters used the lobby as a break room while they were fighting the fires at Ground Zero. Each day now, we go check on every apartment on every floor—294 apartments on thirty-three floors. We go up and down the stairs in the dark, checking on pets and watching for looters."

"Bless you for doing all that for everyone," Brian said. "Amazing. Thank you so much!"

"That's so noble, really—a noble act," I added. "I'm sure your families wanted you home. Surely you wanted to go home, too. This was so far beyond the call of duty."

Gus blushed. "Well, I know that the staff of other buildings nearby did the same."

Feeling better about the fate of our apartment, we borrowed a flashlight from Gus, put on white face masks, and began to climb the same stairs we had rushed down after the second plane hit. The smell of smoke permeated the stairwell, and dust was thick in the air. We were alone in total darkness except for the beam from the flashlight. It took us a half hour to get up the twenty-four flights of stairs, since I had to rest a lot. Finally, we opened the heavy exit door and stepped into the darkness of our hallway.

We stopped in front of our front door, where Brian prayed, "Lord, let us be OK no matter what we find. Thank you so much for watching over us." Then he opened the door.

I blinked, my eyes adjusting to the bright sunlight pouring through the windows and open terrace doors. The light revealed a yellow-hued wonderland. Dust and small pieces of random debris covered every surface—the couch, the desk, the dining room table, the kitchen countertops. The sun's rays reflected off of the dust like fallen snow, setting the apartment aglow.

"Wow, Brian! Look at this!" I said, surprised and relieved. I had been worried that we would find a charred black space with everything broken or burned.

We walked carefully around the apartment, feeling like we had stepped onto another planet. Ironically, on the coffee table in front of our sofa was *The Alienist*, the book I'd been reading before we evacuated. I picked it up, leaving a perfect book-sized dust outline on the table.

I ventured into the bedroom. Sifting through the dust on the nightstand, I located my wedding ring, right where I had left it, and slipped it on. I took our wedding portrait off the wall and slid it under the bed, then looked closely around the bedroom and bathroom before making my way back into the living room. Brian was taking files from his desk drawers.

"I am *shocked* that everything is intact," I marveled. "Nothing here appears broken, and nothing seems missing. Have you noticed anything?"

"No, everything's here," he answered, thumbing through papers. "This is a surreal zombie apartment."

I suddenly noticed a bizarre mass in the southeastern corner of the living room, right next to the dining room table. What looked from a distance to be a papier-mâché sculpture turned out to be a large pile of charred papers. The wind must have swept them in over the past four days, creating a congealed glob that stood almost four feet high.

"All this stuff must have come straight from the towers. I wish I had time to sort through it right now."

Although our home was in better condition than I had expected, it was definitely unlivable. Nothing in the apartment—from clothes to books to kitchen appliances—appeared salvageable. The soot and fine dust had penetrated everything. And yes, the terrace doors were open. Maybe Gus or someone else had tried to close the doors, but our quirky doors would not stay closed unless they were dead-bolted. I walked onto the terrace, but debris forced me to stay close to the doors.

Looking toward where the World Trade Center used to be, I could see the smoking hole of Ground Zero—visible because of missing pieces in buildings that once had obscured my view of the bottom of the towers. I felt as if I were out on a stranger's terrace looking over a strange city. I barely recognized anything, and I began to weep.

Hearing Brian rustling inside, however, snapped me back into reality.

I can't dwell on this now. And if stay here, I'll totally lose it.

I moved back inside and found Brian checking on the faucets.

"I found Gaby's vet records, got our Social Security cards and birth certificates, picked up our cell phones, and our laptops."

My hero.

I rushed back into the bedroom and grabbed a few pieces of clothing for Brian and me, and picked up my purse with my wallet. As I walked toward the front door, Brian closed and locked the terrace doors.

Twenty minutes after we first stepped into our apartment, we began making our way back down the stairs.

Returning the flashlight to Gus, Brian asked, "Any news on when we'll be able to get back into Le Rivage?"

"Officials need to come to every building in the area to make sure they're structurally sound," Gus replied. "They haven't come to 21 West, yet."

"Guess that means it could be a while. Well, I'm so glad we got to get in the apartment for a few minutes anyway. Thanks for the help, Gus, and for taking such good care of the building!"

As we walked away, I began to obsess about what might be lurking in the thick layers of dust in our apartment. We had read multiple articles with conflicting explanations since the attacks. Although the Environmental Protection Agency had announced that there were "no significant levels of asbestos" in the dust, other officials and scientists had warned of "multiple hazardous toxins."

Back on the subway, I told Brian that I had heard some people had refused to evacuate. "How could anyone be living down there? The area's a no-man's land. Smoke and debris are everywhere, electricity is off, all the stores are closed. Everything in their refrigerator's gone bad. What do they even have to eat? I don't see how—or why—anyone would make that choice."

"I know why," Brian said slowly. "They want to be home. They love their home. Even with all this, they feel safest in their home."

I began to tear up.

"Brian, we don't know what's going to happen to our home.

We might have no home to go back to, if the building is declared structurally unsound. And our place is a mess. We will have to start over."

"Let's just take it day by day," my husband replied wisely.

That's it. That really is all I need to do. Try to concentrate on each day. We'll think about our future later. We don't have to make any decisions on anything soon. I'll try to channel Scarlett O'Hara: "I'll think about it tomorrow. After all, tomorrow is another day!"

Then I remembered that a few hours ago I had been desperate just to see our apartment and was overwhelmed with a sense of gratitude that we had managed to get into the Frozen Zone.

I have peace of mind that no more damage will be done to our home because the doors are shut. I've seen our place, and I know what we're dealing with. I have my wedding ring, purse, and ID, and Brian got our phones and computers. I'm sure not worried about looters any more. If they're going to brave that mess and chaos, go right on ahead. Take it all, robbers!

The moment of gratitude brought a sigh of relief. Followed almost immediately by a sickening feeling in the pit of my stomach and a thought that flashed into my head out of nowhere: *I'm not sure I WANT to go back there and live anymore.*

I tried to push the thought out of my mind.

Returning to Sarah's apartment, we decided to walk to the vet's clinic, briefing Jeff and Sarah about our adventure on the way. As soon as we arrived, the vet pulled Brian and me into a private room while Sarah and Jeff waited in the lobby.

"The dust Gaby licked contained ground-up glass that he ingested. Because of this, he sustained cuts to his esophagus." The vet adjusted his glasses and continued in a flat, yet sympathetic tone. "Terriers are prone to experiencing esophageal issues, and his has been damaged during this ordeal. They are also are predisposed to having brachycephalic syndrome, another condition affecting short-nosed dogs, which can lead to severe respiratory distress. I believe breathing in the dust that day affected his respiratory system, too. Lastly, Gaby has cuts on his eyes, due to the glass particles in the dust. We need to attend to that as well."

As the vet rattled off the list of ailments, I wondered if Gaby would survive.

But the vet seemed cautiously optimistic. "I'm not recommending surgery at this point," he advised. "Just keep a close eye on Gaby, and we'll revisit that idea in a week if he hasn't improved." He prescribed antibiotics, other medications to treat the esophageal inflammation and pain, and ointment for his eyes. We collected Gaby, as well as our $517 vet bill, and Brian carried him back to Sarah's apartment, where he promptly threw up and then sank back into his lethargic state.

The harrowing journey to our apartment and the news about Gaby had exhausted me. I had no appetite and just wanted to go to bed. Right before I climbed the ladder to the top bunk, I turned on the computer we had retrieved from our apartment.

There were almost thirty emails from friends and family wanting to know how we were doing. It made me feel so loved! But I didn't have the energy to answer each one individually, so I created a cut-and-paste message, which I tried to make sound more chipper and positive than I actually felt.

"Thanks so much for thinking of us! Brian and I feel lucky to be alive. . . . ."

11

Wounded and Walking:
September 15 and 16

"HEY YA'LL—I'M GOING OUT! See you later," I yelled as I shut the apartment door behind me. I had seen a flyer advertising free food and clothing at a nearby Salvation Army. I decided Saturday morning was a good time to go and investigate.

Restaurant bills and the cost of the food and toiletries from the local bodega were adding up. Brian and I also needed more clothes to supplement what I had brought from the apartment and the pieces we had borrowed from Sarah and Jeff. We had no idea how long we would be out of our home, so we needed to start planning for more than just our daily needs.

I strolled across 46th Street through Hell's Kitchen and entered into a dark, grubby-looking Salvation Army warehouse.

Toiletries, food, and clothing were piled into high peaks, all neatly subdivided into mini-mountains. I guess the reports I had heard about New Yorkers overwhelming donation depots were no joke!

"Can I help you?" a friendly volunteer approached me.

"Oh, hi, I need some pants for my husband and me," I responded awkwardly.

"Follow me. We can look for them together."

Whoa. For the first time in my life I'm on the receiving end of a volunteer effort. I've volunteered my entire life at places like these. There's no shame in needing help. But am I taking things away from someone else who needs it more?

I put my misgivings aside and picked out some clothing I

thought we could use. Then I asked the young woman if I could also get some food.

"Of course," she responded, leading me to a narrow side room with long shelves of food, cleaning supplies, toiletries, and baby gear. "You're welcome to get what you need," she said, leaving me in the room. I filled my backpack.

I ran all the way back to Sarah's apartment—eager to show off my booty.

I'm going to look for more places like that one! I've got plenty of time to travel around and pick up free stuff. Maybe I can begin a new career as a "hunter-gatherer."

I woke Brian when I returned. "Look at all these things I got for us today!" I proudly displayed the pants, three tubes of toothpaste, a jar of spaghetti sauce, two cans of cream of mushroom soup, and a box of maxi-pads.

"That's nice," Brian responded, then turned back over on the bed. His lethargic response didn't squelch my manic excitement. Rustling through flyers I'd gathered, I sat down and made a schedule for the upcoming week.

I'll go to the Salvation Army on 14th Street and search for hair products and dog food. Then maybe to that thrift store on East 17th that's giving away clothes—that one requires people to have a Lower Manhattan address. Then I could head on over to the back of the Jacob Javits Convention Center for cans of meat and fresh vegetables.

I knew I didn't have to scavenge for all our supplies—we were not *that* short on money. But I was excited by the prospect of leaving the apartment with a destination and goal in mind. I needed something to *do.*

Brian, Gaby, and I had the apartment mostly to ourselves all day. Sarah was working a waitressing shift, and Jeff had returned to his apartment in Brooklyn. Brian and Gaby both slept most of the day.

I watched the news while reading and answering emails. But I could not find a way to make my messages sound chipper today. "I'm so upset and I feel so unglued. I am just not myself. This is all so awful," I wrote to a friend from Raleigh.

After watching the news alone for a few hours, I took Gaby out, then decided to walk for a while to burn off energy. I knew Gaby couldn't keep up, so I returned him to the apartment and stepped back outside.

Brian's still asleep. No one will miss me. I can be gone the rest of the day if I want to.

And I was.

<hr />

The next morning, Brian asked, "Christina, do you want to go to church today? I don't know where we'd go. But we need to go somewhere."

Brian and I had visited a few churches since we had returned to New York, but none were near Sarah's apartment.

"I just don't feel like it this morning, Brian," I responded. "I have no decent clothes, I have no makeup and I look awful. Let's go next Sunday, OK? Maybe I'll feel more presentable and together then." His disappointed reaction made me feel guilty, but it seemed bizarre to do anything I had done prior to Tuesday. It was like my life had been completely upended by the attacks. Or maybe I just wanted to wallow in my present status and wasn't ready to go back to "normal" yet.

After I turned him down, Brian went back to bed. He had been sleeping a lot since our trip to the apartment. So was Gaby. Between his ailments and the medication, Gaby could barely manage a quick bathroom break before he wanted to sleep again.

I felt the urge to walk. I started down 9th Avenue, then took a left at 42nd Street and a right on Broadway. Every block or so, I'd stop to read flyers and look at pictures of the still missing. I soon happened upon a mass in a beautiful Catholic church, the Holy Innocents, on 37th. The doors were open, and I decided to go in.

The place was packed, so I sat down in the last pew and prayed. *Lord, please comfort the families of those who died. Please help them catch who did this so they can't hurt anyone else. Please restore this City. Please watch over Brian and comfort him too. I know I'm supposed to rely on you in times like these, Lord, but I don't really know what that means. I don't really even know how to in normal times. I'm sorry I'm not a stronger Christian.*

In that pew, for the first time since the attacks, I tried to assess where I was spiritually. I wasn't questioning my faith, revisiting Christianity, or asking *why*. I had never been the kind who wanted to blame God for injustice or cataclysmic events. But even though I wanted to talk to God about everything that was happening, I was also feeling very detached from him.

In all honesty, I felt detached from everyone and everything. I just couldn't ponder questions any deeper than what we were going to eat for dinner. It was all too much to bear. Thinking about meals was much easier than remembering the plane ramming into the tower or the chaotic horror in Battery Park.

I relaxed in the beauty of the Gothic church for a while and then left to continue down Broadway. At Union Square Park, I joined a crowd of roughly 200 people gathered near the statue of George Washington on the southern end of the park. This 1856 statue of Washington on a horse was one of my favorites, one I always pointed out to tourists. I was surprised to find so many candles, flags, and flowers piled under the statue that they almost completely covered the twelve-foot granite base. Someone had also wrapped a large flag around the horse's neck and tagged a peace sign on its rump.

A man I assumed was a Native American was chanting and performing some kind of ceremony in front of the statue. His face was painted in vibrant colors, and he wore animal skin pants and a feathered headdress that stretched halfway down his back. His chest and feet were bare. Waving a long stick over the candles and flowers, he swayed and stomped his feet in a dance, while chanting in a language I did not recognize.

He wailed and chanted in low, sustained pitches, clearly communicating straight from his heart, and I gathered that he was praying or reciting a sort of requiem for the people who had died. Tears streamed down his face, and many in the crowd were crying as well. I was deeply moved and, surrounded by all these weeping people, felt a camaraderie and a sense of comfort I had not experienced before. Complete strangers were holding hands and hugging. Our common language was grief, and it was a therapeutic relief. I thought of my prayer in the Catholic church that morning.

I want to feel God's therapeutic love on me! I need Him to help me in whatever way to get through and out of the no-man's land I'm being sucked into.

I slowly walked the two miles back to Sarah's apartment and found Brian sitting on the sofa watching the news. I plopped down next to him, and we watched without speaking. Brian's cell phone rang.

"Hi, Joe!"

I knew he was talking to Joe Mizzi, a fraternity brother from his days at Clemson University. All the color drained from Brian's face and he began shaking. He hung up after a brief conversation.

His voice cracking, Brian said, "Joe told me that Jim White died in the Twin Towers." Brian stopped and caught his breath, still shaking. Jim had also been an Alpha Tau Omega fraternity brother at Clemson. "There will be a memorial service on the twenty-second in Cranbury, New Jersey. Joe invited us to ride with him."

I had never met Jim, but I knew he meant a lot to Brian. "Did you have any idea?"

"I knew he worked in the towers, but I kept hoping that he was out of town that day or that he had made it out in some miraculous way.

I really didn't think I would *know* someone who died in the towers."

Jim had been working for Cantor Fitzgerald, a finance company whose corporate headquarters were located on Floors 101 to 105 of the North Tower, several floors above where the first plane had hit. More than two-thirds of Cantor Fitzgerald employees died that day: 658 people total.

Brian said, "I'm going to bed." It was 6:00 p.m.

Alone, I flipped the channels, looking for a distraction, but every channel was airing something related to the attacks. I turned off the TV and opened my computer, happy to spot an email from a college buddy. But her words confused me: "I'm so glad you live far from there and didn't get caught up in the craziness."

"Live far from there"? What does that mean? She actually visited us right after we moved in. She knows how close I live to the Twin Towers!

I couldn't think of any response.

The next email was a reply from my Raleigh friend, the one I had been honest with. "Why are you so upset? At least you're still alive!"

I slammed the lid on my laptop and sat immobilized, feeling completely overwhelmed. But I couldn't sit still so decided to go for another walk.

I walked for three hours through Midtown. I had walked for hours over the past two days, covering many miles in my flimsy BJ's flip-flops, but I still couldn't turn myself "off."

I felt like I was trying to walk away from my own mind.

12

Anger, Anxiety Overtake Grief: September 17 and 18

ON MONDAY, I WOKE long before Brian and Sarah and headed straight to the TV. Each day brought revelations about how the heck this had happened and what would happen next. During a commercial break, Mayor Giuliani appeared with several Broadway stars to encourage viewers to head back to the theater. "Go see a Broadway show! Hey, now you can get that ticket to *The Producers* you've been waiting to see."

Huh. I've never seen that before. Performers basically begging people to go to Broadway. Wow, this must be a very tough time for actors. I can't imagine getting up on a stage, putting on a big smile, and performing with all this going on right outside the stage doors. I'm night and day away from that world now. And I have no desire to be a part of it.

That last thought surprised me. It was the first time I had ever *not* wanted to be a part of the Broadway scene.

When the news coverage returned, I was surprised to see a video from 9/11 of people boarding a boat. "Hey! That's what happened to us! The boat evacuation!" I said aloud. This was the first report I had seen about how boats had rescued people from Battery Park that morning. I strained to see if I could see Brian and myself, but we weren't in the footage. The news anchor told the story as the video played.

> Boats began picking people up in Lower Manhattan while the towers were still burning. When word got out that hundreds, then thousands, of people were pooling at the tip of Manhattan, the US Coast

Guard got involved. They issued a radio call asking boats to help take people off the island to a place of safety. The Coast Guard wasn't sure if any boat would respond, but they did. By the hundreds. After just one radio call, the coastline of Lower Manhattan began to fill with boats of every size and shape. Some of them traveled back and forth all day across the Hudson and East Rivers and NY Harbor, transporting people away from the attack zone. Five hundred thousand people were rescued in less than nine hours. It is considered to be the largest sea evacuation in history.

The boats dropped people off all over the New York metro area. Some went to Brooklyn, some to Staten Island, some to New Jersey, some to Upper Manhattan.

I was surprised by the report, particularly by how many people had been rescued from that area: 500,000 people! And I was also surprised to learn that we had not all been dropped off in the same place. I hoped other evacuees got a more helpful welcome than we had received in Paulus Hook!

After a few hours watching the news by myself, I felt antsy and was ready to head out on my daily rounds of hunting for giveaways. I was still sporting those flimsy flip-flops from BJ's Wholesale Club, and my feet had started to hurt. I planned to head first for a donation station to get new tennis shoes and decided to wear Brian's sneakers for the trip. He was still sleeping, and I knew he wouldn't be leaving the apartment when he did get up.

Brian's shoes were two sizes too big for me and well past their prime, but they would be more comfortable than those flip-flops. As I walked, I began to notice a disgusting odor. I assumed it came from the mountains of trash bags lining the sidewalks, but the smell remained even after I turned onto an empty side street.

I realized it must be me. I stopped and smelled my pits, my shirt, then my shorts, but couldn't find the source. The smell was awful—something rancid, putrid. The only thing I hadn't checked? My feet. I sat down on the edge of the sidewalk, took off my right shoe, and smelled my foot. It didn't seem too bad, but a whiff of the shoe made me gag. It was the *shoes!* But the odor was the smell of a dead animal, not stinky feet.

Suddenly, I realized exactly what was causing the odor. Brian had been wearing these shoes on 9/11 when we ran through the clouds of gunk in Battery Park, and I knew without a shadow of a doubt that the odor was coming from decomposing human remains on the shoes.

I got up from the curb and ran the twelve blocks to the Javits Donation Center. Arriving out of breath and semi-hysterical, I blurted to the receptionist, "I need sneakers right away. Anything you got. Size 9 or 10—something like that. I'll take anything."

"The shoe section is right over there." She pointed to the right hand corner. "Go pick out whatever you want."

I quickly picked out a pair for each of us, and switched into my new shoes immediately, then ran outside and tossed Brian's old sneakers into a trash can. I sat down on the curb and tried to calm down.

I'm so grossed out. Just....I mean what the hell?! But I'm all the way down here. I should continue with my errands. I should go back in and get the other things we need. Anything that gets this off my mind.

As I went back inside, I noticed a sign taped to the entrance: "We are accepting no more volunteers." I walked to the reception table and saw bored-looking volunteers sitting, standing, and leaning against the walls. About eight ran over as I approached.

"A bottle of shampoo, please," I asked.

All of them ran to the back of the room to get one for me. Looking around, I realized volunteers outnumbered those of us looking for donations by about fifteen to one. I no longer felt any shame about letting volunteers serve me—I knew I had legitimate needs and was now willing to let other people help fill those needs.

Leaving the Javits, I walked aimlessly for the rest of the day. Block after block, avenue after avenue. When I finally returned home, I told Brian, "Hey, hon, I got you some new shoes and I chucked the old ones. That OK?"

He shrugged and thanked me, clearly not caring one way or the other. I didn't tell Brian—or anyone—about the odor on the shoes. It was just too traumatizing to verbalize.

On Tuesday, exactly one week after the attacks, I got up to find Sarah preparing to go to an audition. She turned to me. "You know what I did last night? I saw a Broadway show! I wanted you to come but you were out walking."

"Really?" How was it?"

"I've never experienced anything like it before, Christina," she said excitedly. "Maybe the theater was only a quarter full. But I couldn't believe how electric the audience was! The night began with the orchestra playing the national anthem and ended with 'God Bless America.' We all bawled throughout the show. . . . ."

Sarah continued to talk about her theater experience, but my mind wandered.

Ya know, to be an actress, you need to be very driven and a good self-promoter, 'cause you're constantly auditioning and jockeying for jobs. It's cool. I'm used to it. I never minded it before. But I cannot imagine hustling right now. I have definitely lost my hustle. I seriously doubt I could conjure it up. Certainly not for performing. I can barely hustle for groceries.

Sarah left for her audition, and I was left with my thoughts. Brian was sleeping again.

I set out on a three-mile "manic walk" all the way to the East Village. I zig-zagged down various streets, moving from west to east. At Madison and 24th, I ran across people lined up to donate blood.

On the corner of 14th and 3rd, four men were loudly arguing.

"Let's go bomb the hell out of 'em!"

"That won't solve anything!"

"We need new laws in this country to make sure this doesn't happen again."

"What exactly would those laws be?"

A crowd was gathering around the men. Some people in the crowd were chiming in while others, like me, just listened. In the past couple of days, I realized that rage was replacing sorrow in the streets. Rage at the terrorists, rage at the countries that produced them, rage that our government had been too slow to react to the warnings they apparently received leading up to the attacks. People wanted justice. People wanted revenge.

I remembered watching President Bush at Ground Zero a few days after the attacks, saying, "I can hear you! The rest of the world hears you! And the people—and the people who knocked these buildings down will hear all of us soon!" I wanted to believe the president. But I wasn't sure there was a punishment big enough to fit this crime.

When I reached the East Village, I noticed a line outside a storefront and learned it was a gallery with photographs of the attacks. I joined the line and waited for about half an hour to enter the tiny commercial space. On the white walls were about thirty framed snapshots, a collection from amateur photographers who had captured the horror of the day from their perspectives.

Several photos were of the burning towers, taken from different angles. There were also close-ups of people witnessing the horror. But the photos I was drawn to the most were the ones that were also the most difficult to look at—people jumping from the towers, crumpled bodies, severed limbs.

Although it felt invasive and inappropriate to stare at these photos, I could not look away. One showed people running away from a severed arm lying on the street. New Yorkers could not grasp the reality of a bloody, severed limb in the middle of a busy Manhattan street. It made no sense. Not in the twenty-first century. As I exited, I noticed the gallery owner sitting near the front door watching everyone view the photos. His grim expression matched everyone else's.

Outside, I debated the appropriateness of the pop-up gallery. Were those photos disrespectful? Voyeuristic? Ultimately, I decided the gallery was really another venue for remembering and communal mourning.

There's value in shared grief. People need comforting, and it's a form of it. But boy, that was upsetting as all get-out.

~~~

I grabbed a *New York Post* and headed into a McDonald's. Paging through the *Post*, I zeroed in on an article about air quality in Lower Manhattan: "Administrator of the Environmental Protection Agency Christine Todd Whitman stated that the EPA had set up seventeen air monitoring stations in Lower Manhattan. The result of the stations' findings has led to the conclusion that the air quality is safe."

I didn't believe it for a second.

I was just down there. There's no way on this earth that the thick dust covering everything, the grit collected in our apartment, the stuff that was on Gaby's fur is safe. If it's so safe, why did my Kleenex turn black when I blew my nose?

Brian and I had not heard that our building had been declared safe, and I was feeling more and more reluctant to return to our apartment. Anytime I thought about being back in our place, my stomach would hurt. I had been reassuring myself that we wouldn't be going back any time soon, but here was this EPA bigwig indicating that the air quality was not a major reason for maintaining the Frozen Zone.

I moved on to the middle of the newspaper and came upon a section called "Help and Hotlines." It was a two-page, side-by-side directory with headings such as "Missing Persons," "Donations," "Aid to Businesses," "Tourists," and "School Information." It was a master list of services for every kind of situation people were facing in the aftermath of 9/11. There were lists of places people could go to volunteer, seek insurance assistance, call in tips to the FBI, or get assistance from the Federal Emergency Management Association (FEMA). Organizations were offering free office space for displaced companies, and at least one real estate company, Citi Habitats, was offering to match displaced persons with NYC residents who had spare bedrooms. I tore that page out of the paper and put it in my backpack.

When I returned to Sarah's apartment late in the afternoon, Brian was watching TV again, but he was dressed as if he'd been out and about. "Hi, hon!" I kissed him. "Did you go somewhere?"

"Yes. I went to fill out FEMA forms today. I'm not sure it can help us, but anything is better than nothing."

I could tell Brian's expectations were as low as mine, but I was happy he had submitted the forms—and happy to hear that my friend Jennifer had called from South Florida.

When I called back, she was surprised to learn I was not living in my own apartment.

"Jennifer, when the Twin Towers came down, they registered on the Richter scale like an earthquake. Our building—along with many, many others—has to be tested to see if it's structurally sound because they were shaken from their foundations. You didn't hear this?"

"No," she responded. "Nothing of the kind. How long have you been out of your home?"

Why doesn't she know this stuff? She's a smart, well-read girl. Is the news in Florida not covering these details?

I made an excuse to cut the conversation short. I appreciated her interest but didn't feel like explaining any more. I sat down to read emails, but couldn't muster any interest in the chatty messages from friends who wanted to tell me about normal life events.

An out-of-state relative wrote, "Are stores closed where you live?! How have tours been going?"

I began to write a response. "Are you kidding? There's no tour-guiding work! The only tourists still here are desperately trying to get the hell out. Yes, lots of stores are closed—like about 18,000 small businesses that were destroyed or displaced—a lot more was damaged than just the World Trade Center complex!"

I shut down the computer before I went any further, fearing I had said too much already. Do people not know what's going on here?

13

An Unexpected Haven:
September 19 and 20

I GROGGILY CLIMBED DOWN from my seventh night on the top bunk and headed to the bathroom. I stepped in something wet along the way and realized Gaby had peed on the floor—again.

In the bathroom, I examined myself in the mirror and winced. I had never struggled with serious skin issues even as a teen, but in the past week, I had developed full-blown acne. The dust and smoke had penetrated my pores, and large, stubborn zits had emerged all over my face. My natural brunette roots had grown out so that the top half of my head was dark brown, and the bottom half was blond. I had missed my September 14 appointment for an extra-special cut and color that I had scheduled in advance of the "housewarming/newlywed party/birthday party" we had been planning for September 22. The party wouldn't be happening now.

I put on the clothes I'd brought from the bedroom and, for the first time since the attacks, really looked at what I was wearing. I'm a curvy girl and very high-waisted, so I can't just pull something off a rack and know it will look good on me. But donation centers weren't exactly known for their dressing rooms, so I had amassed a small collection of ill-fitting donated clothes. My mother, who prefers tailored, smart clothing, would have thrown a fit if she'd seen what I was wearing.

But I saw no reason to spend money on clothes or hair care— what I saw in the mirror reflected exactly what I was feeling inside. I was walking zombie-like around town for hours at a time, and

I had not slept well in days. I just didn't care how I looked, and I didn't have the energy to take care of myself. I moved on to the kitchen, where I poured a cup of coffee and plopped down on a chair by the tiny table. I knew Sarah was gone because her red backpack wasn't in its normal spot. I hadn't seen much of her since Friday's adventure to Pier 40. When I wasn't out on one of my crazy walks, she was either working, in her room, or visiting Jeff in Brooklyn. Brian continued to sleep most of the day and spent his few waking hours in front of the TV.

Feeling lost, I decided to call Mom.

She answered quickly. "How are you?"

"I don't know, Mom. I feel like things have shifted since Saturday, the day after we went to our apartment and got Gaby from the vet. Brian is sleeping all the time, and I can't sleep at all. I'm on high alert, jumpy. Like, I feel I'm still on guard for the next threat. We're both in such a funk. Brian and I aren't talking much at all. When we do, we just talk about silly things like what we're going to eat. We never, ever talk about the attacks. It's become kinda taboo."

After listening quietly, my mother said, "Yes, I've noticed on the phone you've seemed hyper and couldn't quit talking. You're on overdrive. As for you and Brian—I think your bodies are both acting out due to the stress. You're just having different reactions. Give yourself a break—you're still newlyweds, you've only been married a year and a half! You met and married quickly. You had no idea how the other responded to drama. Even predictable drama. You have no history—no frame of reference for all this."

"Yeah," I agreed, recognizing the wisdom in my mother's words. "Brian and I had been so action-oriented since last Tuesday morning. We had to be just to survive that day. But after that visit to our apartment, and attending to Gaby's health, there's nothing to *do* anymore."

"I think you should get out of your environment," Mom said.

"You sound stuck. You can't even begin to heal. Why don't you come home to Tallahassee?"

Mom's words comforted me somewhat, but I simply couldn't contemplate heading to Florida right now. It would require more effort than I could muster, and somehow I thought it would also be an admission of defeat. But even a small change of scenery might be good for us.

I tiptoed into the bedroom and found Brian awake.

"Brian, it might be time to consider looking for another place to stay," I told him. "I'm feeling cramped. Gaby's making a mess, and it embarrasses me. I can't sleep either. The top bunk is uncomfortable and the truck noise on 9th Avenue is awful. Can I look into alternatives?"

I didn't mention the obvious big picture issues—that he was sleeping all the time and I couldn't sit still and we had no long-term plans.

Brian nodded his blessing, though I sensed he was skeptical we could find an affordable option. We didn't know whether it would be two weeks or two months before we got back into our apartment. Or ever. I'm an actress and tour guide and Brian was job-searching before the attacks, and any kind of work was probably going to be hard to come by for a while since so many businesses had been destroyed or forced to shut down.

I tried to think of any other friends who might have a spare room or be out of town. Suddenly, I remembered the housing ad I had seen in the *Post*. I retrieved the torn-out page and reread the notice: "Citi Habitats Emergency Housing Help Center is open 9 am–8 pm to help those displaced find temporary accommodations. Some are free, others cost a nominal fee. Call 212 692-7777." It seemed a little weird—what New Yorker would host strangers off the street? We could wind up someplace a lot worse than Sarah's.

I called anyway.

A woman answered, and I blurted out everything at once. "My name is Christina and I'm calling about your ad regarding the opportunity to stay in donated housing; my husband and I live in the Financial District and we've been displaced since September 11th; is there anyone offering free accommodations? Oh, we also have a small dog."

The woman took down the necessary details and promised to get back to me.

I hung up feeling nervous and pessimistic, but she called back an hour later. "There is a studio possibility near Grand Central Terminal, and the owner, Jodi Stewart, would not be present if you stayed there. There would be no charge, and bringing your dog is fine." She gave me the owner's number and said, "If things don't work out for any reason, call us back."

Surprised and elated, I ran to give Brian the news. "Do you mind contacting her? You're better at thinking through any logistical stuff."

"Sure, I'll do it," Brian said, picking up the phone.

After a short conversation, Brian said, "Turns out she's a young woman who's engaged and lives in a small studio apartment on the ground floor of her building. She plans to go up to Connecticut for a while with her fiancé to get out of the City. She says we're welcome to use the apartment, but she wants to meet with us first—or at least one of us. I set up a meeting with her tomorrow."

"Oh wow, great! This is kind of an adventure, isn't it, Brian?"

He gave me a wry smile that I interpreted as, "Please. I'm adventured out!"

Brian left about 9:30 on Thursday morning to meet with Jodi, but I couldn't work up the energy to go with him. My manic meanderings had been a great outlet for my energy overload and allowed me to engage in the City's collective mourning. But the mania was easing, and I felt completely drained.

Brian returned in a little over an hour. "We talked for a little bit and she asked to see my ID to make sure I was 'legit,' I guess. She gave me the key, and that was that!"

"Yay!" I yelled, incredulous and ecstatic. "Let's leave right away!"

I called Sarah at work to tell her about our opportunity and was relieved that she was understanding. I certainly didn't want Sarah to feel like we were rejecting her after all she had done for us!

I rooted through the apartment, collecting clothing and toiletries I had gathered from donation depots around town, and threw them into a few plastic bags. I was still marveling that someone—a New Yorker, no less—was offering her home to complete strangers without a background check, referral, or payment of any kind.

Thank you, God, for this angel, Jodi!

We leashed up Gaby and walked the mile to Jodi's charming 500-square-foot studio. Even though it was on the ground floor, we couldn't hear a sound from outside. No more Hell's Kitchen truck noise to keep me awake at night! The apartment was sparsely furnished but clean and bright, and it had a queen-sized bed. No more top bunk!

I turned on the TV, and we sank into a futon. Brian was smiling for the first time in days. Even Gaby seemed to be perking up. It had been almost a week since he'd been to the vet, and he was slowly getting better. I felt more hopeful than I had in days as I settled into this unexpected haven.

14

Stunning News:
September 21

As we watched the news on Friday, we heard the anchor explain something that had baffled us for days. "Investigators have determined that both of the towers imploded instead of toppling over, resulting in countless saved lives. Each floor was an acre, and 110 floors were equal to one-quarter mile in height. If the towers had fallen lengthways in any direction, they would have killed many more people on the ground. If the South Tower had fallen south, it would have stretched to the northern boundary of Battery Park."

Brian looked up from his laptop and said, "We sure thought they were going to fall on us, didn't we?"

"Yup. Us and everyone else. If we could have seen them implode, that crazy scene down in Battery Park probably wouldn't have felt so terrifying."

"Yeah, but there was too much smoke and dust in the air to be able to tell exactly what was happening," said Brian. "I've also realized from some of the news I've seen that we weren't as trapped as we felt. There probably were several escape routes we could have taken to walk out of that danger."

We were both quiet. Knowing now that our situation had not been as dire as it seemed on 9/11 did nothing to erase the terror of those hours.

The TV anchor continued describing what had happened that day. "The unique resonation of the falling towers was the result of air being forced out of the 110 floors as each story was flattened like a pancake from the floors above."

"I had been wondering about that strange-sounding noise," I said. What I didn't say was how much that weird, horrible, ear-splitting, avalanche-type sound had replayed in my mind ever since the attacks.

Brian looked back at his computer. "Christina, listen to this email I just got: '21 West has been declared structurally sound, the asbestos levels in the Financial District have been checked and were very low, the electricity is back on, and the building is fully operational.' Christina, we can go home!"

"What?"

We sat for a minute, shocked. I broke the silence. "It's the twenty-first. *It's ten days after the deadliest terrorist attack on American soil in US history. Which happened just six blocks away from our apartment. This is insanity!*"

"It seems very premature to imagine people can return to their homes and jobs in Lower Manhattan," Brian agreed. "The entire area near Ground Zero seemed incapable of supporting a decent quality of life anytime in the near future."

"I mean, c'mon! It's still on fire down there! They just said on the news that almost two million tons of debris are spread over sixteen acres of devastation. So, how are all of us who live there supposed to get from point A to point B? Sidestepping debris and fires in the middle of our neighborhood?"

Brian voiced other concerns. "The search for human remains is still going on around the clock. Wouldn't having us back disturb this work? And I just read that 23,000 Lower Manhattan apartments have to be cleaned and tested for asbestos. Certainly that isn't finished yet!"

"I know! I mean, how the heck did they do all that already?" I stood up, my voice rising as I grew more and more upset. "Dust is still in the air. What are we supposed to do—hold our breath? This is crazy!"

Sitting back down suddenly, I added quietly, "And dang it—we just got here!" I was becoming panicky, and my stomach began to hurt.

Lord, I don't want to go home! I'm not ready. I don't feel well enough to handle it. I'm scared. I'm worried that the dark force I saw and felt is still there. But I don't want Brian to know how I feel. I would hate for him to think that his wife is rejecting the home he was so proud of securing. It's not fair to him, after all he's been through. Lord, help me cope with this.

"Well," he answered, rereading the email. "The EPA says that 'Lower Manhattan is ready to welcome everyone back.' The area must be in better shape for the apartment management to give us the green light to return. Imagine the liability if they told us we could come back prematurely! And here's good news: We won't be charged rent from September eleventh to the thirtieth. So, the management is giving us a rent break, which is great.

"It looks like it's time to go back home, Christina. Let's do it Sunday."

I took a deep breath. "OK. But I don't like it." I knew better than most that nothing slows New York City for long. Over the years, I'd taken tour groups to the Statue of Liberty during snowstorms—even the 1996 blizzard—because, well, the boats were still running, and it was still open. When a bomb exploded in the World Trade Center in 1993, killing six and wounding 1,000, people were back to work at the complex within days. The City just keeps going.

I was extremely skeptical that our neighborhood was ready to welcome us back, but I decided to trust our building's management, the mayor, the City, the EPA, and President Bush. Brian had a point. It was time to face the music. And face whatever was making me not want to return.

Lord, please help me adjust. Please help with my anxiety.

Returning to Le Rivage on Sunday would be a challenge in

more ways than one. But we had another milestone to concentrate on between then and now, and I worried it would be the most difficult undertaking of all since the attacks: attending Jim's memorial service.

Brian, Gaby, and me: Our first Christmas together as a married couple (2000) in Raleigh, North Carolina. About six months later, we moved back to NYC.

On the steps of First Baptist Church, Tallahassee, Florida, on our wedding day, March 18, 2000.

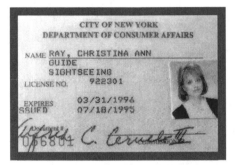

My first NYC tour guide license.

The Observation Deck
TOP OF THE WORLD
AT THE WORLD TRADE CENTER

New York City's One and Only Multilingual Interactive Attraction
Glass Enclosed Observatory & Outdoor Viewing Platform

- Free Multilingual Interactive Video Monitors
- Gift Shops - New York City Novelties & Souvenirs
- Picnic Dining, Catered Events & Private Functions

HOURS:
9:30 a.m. - 9:30 p.m. (September - May)
9:30 a.m. - 11:30 p.m. (June - August)

Tel: (212)323-2340
Fax: (212)323-2352

Original ticket for the observatory.

Original World Trade Center Observation Deck brochure.

My dear friend Michelle, who urged me to ask for financial assistance from Redeemer.

Jeff and Sarah and us in 2018: The shared experience of 9/11 helped strengthen our friendship.

My mother and me.

Wedding photos by Lois Griffin

Our building in proximity to the towers. The Hudson River is in the foreground, where we boarded a boat and evacuated to New Jersey.

Our north-facing view from the terrace. On the day of the attacks, we saw fire trucks, police cars, and ambulances race down the West Side Highway to the burning towers while people ran across it to escape the danger.

Our night view from our terrace.

A photo taken on the day of our journey through the "Frozen Zone" to our apartment.

On our "Frozen Zone" trek. Notice our ill-fitting donated clothing, face masks, and the debris on the car.

One of the several flyer collections of missing people that were pasted on edifices all over town.

A leaflet listing shelters for people who lived in the "Frozen Zone" and who were now homeless as a result.

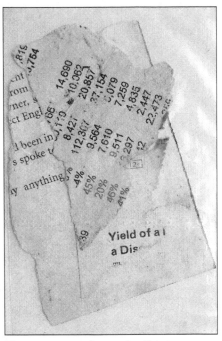

These are scraps of paper that flew into our apartment from the Twin Towers and became a part of the papier-mâché sculpture.

The first photo taken from the terrace after returning to our apartment on Sept. 23. The black Deutsche Bank building is in the foreground. You can also see a corner chunk dangling off of one of the World Financial Center buildings.

The names of Jim (James) and his girlfriend, Amy, side by side on the 9/11 memorial. Jim was Brian's fraternity brother at Clemson, and we went to his memorial service.

The only picture I have of Brian and me on our terrace with the towers in the background.

A picture of myself and Dr. Timothy Keller, the founding pastor of Redeemer Presbyterian Church—the church we began attending after 9/11. This church helped transform our lives, and Brian and I continue to work for the church as short-term missions director and CFO.

For more photos, visit: christinaraystanton.com

15

Crushing Sorrow:
September 22

SATURDAY, SEPTEMBER 22, 2001, was my thirty-second birthday. It was also the date we had been planning to hold our "house-warming/newlywed/birthday party" at our new apartment.

But instead of heading out for a fun day with Brian or preparing for a party, we left Jodi's place with Brian's friend Joe, who drove us to Cranbury, New Jersey, for Jim White's memorial service.

On the church's front steps, Brian and Joe greeted fraternity brothers who had traveled from around the country to attend the service. I was deeply touched at this show of support. A portrait of Jim at the front of the Catholic church showed a thin, good-looking man with a kind smile, a twinkle in his eye, and short brown hair. An everyday man. Jim had been thirty-four years old.

It was strange not to see a casket at the church, but no remains had been found. At that very moment, workers were sifting through the debris at Ground Zero, searching for identifiable remains of thousands of people.

Jim's dad got up to speak first, followed by a brother and a friend. As they spoke, I began to feel like I had known Jim too. "Jim was a practical joker, full of personality."

"He loved his wild and wacky adventures like running with the bulls in Spain."

"He ran three marathons, played tennis, and was a great skier."

"He always had a smile on his face, and he always had fun."

"Jim was dating a co-worker, twenty-three-year-old Barnard graduate Amy O'Doherty, who had worked for Cantor Fitzgerald for only sixteen months. She died with Jim."

I suddenly remembered hearing Brian talking to Jim on the phone several months ago, planning a double date after we returned to New York.

I had cried very little since 9/11, but in the pew of that church at a service for a man I had never met, I began to sob. And I couldn't stop. Soon my face was completely red, and I was a general mess. The memorial service had finally made me face the magnitude of all those lost lives.

I had an indirect connection to only two of the almost 3,000 people who died on September 11—and I had never even met those two. But suddenly, I felt overcome by the agonizing suffering and grief being experienced by so many people who lost loved ones. And my sorrow clearly contained some release of my own trauma as well.

We were all quiet on the ride back after the service. It was only the second birthday I had marked since I met Brian, and I knew he had intended to take me on a special date to celebrate since we weren't able to have the party we'd initially planned. I usually make a big deal out of my birthday; it's an opportunity to throw a party, and I love parties. But this year I felt too guilty to even think about celebrating. I was alive to turn another year older when Amy and Jim and so many others would never have another birthday. They had been viciously murdered.

"Brian, please let's not do anything for my birthday," I begged as we opened the door to Jodi's apartment. "I just want to go to bed."

He didn't protest. But he gave me a hug and kiss and said, "Happy birthday, hon." It was the only present I got that day, and the only one that mattered.

I'm blessed to have Brian as my partner, blessed that I'm able to enjoy more days of this earthly gift God's given me. Thank you, Lord!

But guilt weighed heavily on me; so many others, like Jim and Amy, had been deprived of what I had been blessed with. Weighed down by sorrow and anxious about returning to our apartment the next day, I spent yet another restless night.

16

Re-Entry into a
Scarred Neighborhood:
September 23

SUNDAY WAS "THE DAY." Just twelve days since 9/11 tore a hole in this City and in our lives, Brian and I were going home.

"I do *not* feel ready to exchange the peace and quiet in Jodi's clean home for the dust, mess, and chaos of our home and neighborhood. Brian, are you sure we can't stay here a few days more? There's plenty of time to get back and get resettled. Does it have to be *right now*? I'm really dreading the clean-up we face."

"There's never going to be a best time to get back and deal with our place, Christina," he responded. The chance to return to our apartment had seemed to re-energize Brian. He wasn't sleeping as much as he had been at Sarah's, and he was clearly ready for this move. "Now is as good a time as any."

"All right, if you think it's the right thing to do."

I made a quick trip to buy a gift for Jodi and her husband-to-be, which we left inside with the key. She had never called or come by to check on us while we were living in her house. I never even met her. We only spent three nights in her apartment, but those three nights had been comforting in ways she could never know, and I was deeply grateful.

"C'mon, we'd better do a grocery run before we get into the subway. We don't know if anything will be open in our neighborhood," Brian wisely advised. Leading Gaby and hauling several heavy plastic bags of donations and groceries, we rode the train to the Bowling Green stop and exited the subterranean terminal. Le Rivage still glowed mustard yellow glow under layers of caked-on dust, but new glass front doors had been installed and the building had been freshly cleaned.

Flo, the concierge, came bounding up. "Hi, Stantons! Welcome back to 21 West! We've missed you!" She gave us both a big hug, and Miguel and Gus came over to shake our hands. My apprehension about returning melted, and I became weepy, grateful that our days of wandering were over.

We took the elevator to the twenty-fourth floor and opened our apartment door. Like a horse being let out of the racing gate, I made a dash straight for the terrace. Brian joined me. He hadn't come outside during our quick trip home, so it was his first time to experience this bewildering view. A gaping hole, plugged by sky, stood where the beautiful, awe-inspiring Twin Towers should be.

Beneath us stretched a panorama of a combat zone. The mounds of debris at Ground Zero opened to devastation and chaos as far as we could see. Cars in the open-air parking garage below us were covered in yellow dust and sprinkled haphazardly with chunks of debris. Many were crushed beyond salvation.

I wonder when the owners are going to come claim those cars. Or will they? How many of the owners died in the attacks?

I shifted my eyes west, toward Battery Park City. A burned-out fire truck had come to rest in a postage-stamp sized park called West Thames. Either it had been blown there by the impact or moved there until it could be dragged to a barge in the Hudson. Near the park, a five-story piece of exterior dangled precariously from a corner of a building in the World Financial Center complex. Directly north of us we could clearly see the multistory, upright piece of facade from the northwest corner of the South Tower, which had become a symbol of the horrific destruction. Dirt and debris and smoldering ashes were visible in every direction. It was ugly, mean, and chaotic, and I still felt the aura of evil that I had first detected on September 11. I shivered, worried the City would be attacked again.

After surveying the scene outside, we took a tour inside our apartment, which was much cleaner than it had been on our last visit. However, an inch of ash and dirt still covered everything, and small mounds of debris were piled up in various corners.

The vertical debris build-up—my "papier-mâché sculpture"—had been reduced to a ten-inch high pile. I abruptly sat down on the floor and began sifting through the scraps, looking for anything personal like a handwritten letter or a photo. But the scraps were tiny, and the ones I could identify appeared to come from accounting books or ledgers. After an hour, I gave up hope of finding anything of significance to anyone else. But I still didn't want to throw them away.

"I should keep 9/11 stuff I've collected and make a scrapbook of it," I told Brian. "I'm sure I'll value this one day." I grabbed a plastic storage bag from the kitchen and filled it with the scraps of paper.

Every floor in our building had laundry facilities, and the management told us we could use them for free until mid-October—a small but significant gesture. We started the process of washing our filthy clothes and linens twice, trying to get the dust out of the fibers. At the same time, we commenced a "purge," throwing out items that had been especially damaged by the smoke and dust.

After a few hours of cleaning, it was time to take Gaby out. He jumped off the couch, seemingly eager to be back on familiar ground. As we walked south down Washington Street, I noticed a sea of canvas tents, the Battery Park campsite for the 750 National Guard troops deployed to assist police and protect against looting.

I was happy to have the troops in the neighborhood, but I was surprised to find that Gaby and I were not allowed in the park.

"You'll need to walk your dog somewhere else," an officer told me.

Finding another suitable place for Gaby was not easy, so we eventually wound up at a dog park area where I had taken Gaby a few times before the attacks. One other dog and owner were present. While our dogs played, she asked, "How is your dog doing? We're so worried about ours. Someone told me they knew two dogs that had died in Battery Park City, and the owner swears it's because of the dust. Supposedly many more are sick. Dogs and cats are close to the ground, so they inhale all that dust and lick it off their feet and fur."

"Really?" I shuddered. "We just returned to the area. This is the first I'd heard of it."

When I returned to our apartment, I was even more aware of all the dust on the floors and the furniture. I grabbed a washcloth and started madly wiping everything down.

17

Living in an Endless Memorial

"BRIAN, WE NEED MORE GROCERIES, and I want to explore around the Financial District to see how it's recovering. Want to come with me?" We had spent most of the past three days cleaning and organizing our apartment, and I needed a change of scenery.

"Great idea!" Brian grabbed his keys.

Everyone we passed in the Financial District was wearing white masks over their noses and mouths. The air still had a weak but distinct smoke and sulpher smell.

"Hmmm . . . maybe we should be wearing masks when we go outside from now on, too." Missing-person flyers and posters were hanging everywhere, with candles and flowers spread on the ground beneath them. Flowers and candles also surrounded charred bikes, which were chained to posts and battered street signs. Missing person flyers were taped on every post of the high fence surrounding the historic St. Paul's Chapel. Brightly colored origami strands were wrapped around every individual spike, along with flags from countries all over the world.

Wow, it's just an endless memorial around here.

On block after block near "the pile"—a new moniker for the sixteen-acre mountain of debris that was still on fire—badly damaged buildings sagged and crumbled, gaping wounds in the tightly built cityscape. Every structure bore signs of trauma. Scraped-up offices and cracked apartment buildings. Battered hotels. The beat-up three-story tenement that housed our local Burger King had been pressed into service as a center for police operations. Black netting covered the Deutsche Bank building.

We didn't spy one unscathed building.

"Man, look at that, Brian. That's the crown jewel of mutilation," I said, pointing at the hollowed-out Deutsche Bank. We strained to look closer at the wreck while leaning as far as we could over the police barricades surrounding Ground Zero. "Do you know what happened to it?"

"Yeah, I read something about it online. When the South Tower collapsed, it tore a twenty-four-story gash into the facade. They placed it under protective black netting until the City decides what to do with it."

"It looks like a gigantic black shroud."

"The reports I read said the rotting building is filled with toxins that are being released into the neighborhood."

"Ugh," I said, staring at the crumbling building. "Incredible. This neighborhood has barely begun the first steps toward recovery."

We had been told it was safe to return to this area, but we found it far from restored. Although there had been some degree of clean-up, reminders of what had happened two weeks earlier were everywhere.

We approached Chelsea Jeans, a retail store that looked like it had been attacked by Godzilla. The business sign had been wrenched off, the front glass window was broken, the glass entryway had been shattered. But people were lined up for a quarter mile, waiting their turn to get inside.

"Brian, let's go in, I want to see what this is. Every time I stand in line at one of these places, I always am glad I did." He nodded, and we joined the back of the line. After a half-hour, we finally made it through the broken doors into a retail house of horrors. Everything in the store was buried in soot and dust. Ash-caked jeans were folded and stacked on tables in the middle of the store and shelves lining the walls—flashes of blue denim occasionally visible through the yellow and gray soot. Dust and debris piled up four inches high on top of hoodies and across the floor. A nasty putrid odor hung as thick as the dust in the air. The store owner stood behind the cash register, peering at the visitors silently filing through.

As we left the store, I said, "I guess he wants to show the world what the attacks did to the Financial District. And his livelihood."

We passed by the boarded-up Rector Street subway entrance. Brian asked, "You heard the Number One subway line next to our building imploded, right?"

"I know," I said glumly. "That was the line I used the most. I hear it will be at least a year before service gets back to Lower Manhattan. That affects thousands of riders!"

But as we walked through block after block of stores behind locked steel gates, I said, "Maybe the missing subway service won't be such a big deal after all. I mean, what is even open? Where are we supposed to shop?

"And the dust! It's everywhere, covering everything." I was almost ranting now. "I mean, how do ya like this? First, they told us it was safe to come back and now they are admitting there might be a *few* dangerous toxins floating around. Maybe! It all makes me nervous!"

Brian tried to calm me. "There are always going to be people spreading scary rumors. But I think that the EPA knows what it's doing. I'm going to trust what it's saying."

"On NBC the other night Tom Brokaw described our neighborhood as 'a nuclear winter.' I think he's right on target. Brian, it's gonna take forever to get all this back into shape. If this had happened in any other part of America, the entire area probably would be abandoned."

"You're probably right—at least to a degree," Brian admitted. "But this is one of the most densely populated cities in the world, and this neighborhood is prime real estate. Not only do thousands of people live here, it also holds the Stock Exchange, and that's very important to all of America. So what if 220 stories collapsed in the middle of it? The City can't stop for long. It has to move as quick as possible to get everything back open."

"I know. But I'm tellin' ya, if this had happened anywhere else, *no one* would be here now. Or for a long time."

As we returned to our apartment, I noticed moving vans parked along the West Side Highway near our building. As we passed Miguel in the lobby, I asked, "Are all those moving vans for our building?"

He answered, "Yes, there are people moving out."

"Miguel, who's left on our floor?"

"Well, out of the six apartments on your floor, three of you stayed."

We took the elevator and walked through an empty hallway back to our apartment. I tried to wipe away the layer of dust that had accumulated in the few hours since I'd last cleaned it away.

"Maybe it's time for us to decide whether to stay or find another place to live," Brian said.

"Let's write down reasons to stay or go, then compare notes!" We both sat and wrote for a half hour. "You go first," I prompted. Brian read his list thoughtfully.

1. I don't want to get out the *Gabriel's Guide* and search again. I'm still getting over being homeless and all that time out of our apartment. I just don't have the energy to go through the apartment-hunting process again.

2. We got our apartment at a good price. We can't find anything better for the price.

3. We're both unemployed, and that should play into the decision. We need to stay put and concentrate on that rather than pulling up stakes and moving.

4. They say they'll get this area up and back in shape soon. They say it's safe and I think they must know what they're talking about.

5. If we leave, the terrorists win. That's my gut reaction right now.

He stopped, and nodded, indicating he was finished. He didn't have a list for why we should leave.

That was Brian, always looking on the bright side. In fact, I had first noticed him on Match.com because of his user name: *consummateoptimist*. It had been one of the first things that drew my attention and one of the traits I had grown to love most about him.

I took a deep breath and rattled off my reasons to stay.

1. I don't want to pack. I hate the idea of packing up and moving again so soon. I'm still not over the experience of leaving a 2,500-square-foot house for an 800-square-foot apartment and a multistate road trip in a U-Haul.

2. I still have a love for this apartment. I still hold out hope it will be our haven—our nest—again soon. Like I thought it was when we first moved in. *But—*

I paused, then read my reasons for why we should go.

1. I don't like living in a war zone. Meaning, I don't like it that everything's closed, transportation's gonna be messed up, and the view from the terrace affects me. It's awful. I hate it.

2. I'm worried about Gaby and his health. And I'm worried about ours too. I disagree with you and the 'experts.' I don't think it's safe.

Putting down my paper, I asked, "Have you heard those rumors about animals getting sick?" We both looked at Gaby.

Brian answered, "Yes. I'm a little nervous about that too. But no vet or official has released any statement making a connection between 9/11 and sick animals. We can't make our decision based on rumors."

I frowned, wishing we knew for sure what was in the dust. But it was pretty clear what we were about to do. "Well, even with the cons I listed, it looks like we both wrote down more reasons to stay. When you get right down to it, we're both just too tired to pack and search for a new place."

I stopped and looked around. "It makes sense," I said slowly, trying to convince myself that it *did* make sense to stay. "We just got here. We went from Raleigh to New York packing and unpacking for two solid months. We'd only been really settled a few days before 9/11. And then, we were gypsies for almost two weeks. It's very hard to find a place to live in New York City—I know how hard you looked for this place, because I did the same for years when I was single. I'm exhausted, and I know you are too. And I don't know about you, but I just want to chill a bit and get my bearings before we make a decision to move on."

Brian nodded vigorously. "I completely agree. We can always reassess in a few weeks." He grabbed my hands and busted out in a spontaneous prayer. "Father, we pray you'll show us what to do. We put our future in your hands. Please give us wisdom. Please watch over us."

"Yes, Lord," I chimed in. "Tell us what to do. Give us strength."

Although we made our decision together, it was still unnerving over the next few days to hear the frequent opening and closing of doors on our hallway, followed by the sound of heavy items being pushed and pulled across the carpet to the elevator outside our door.

18

Relief from Redeemer

On Saturday, September 29, I woke up and realized I had nowhere to go and nothing to do. It was a foreign feeling for me. I walked into the living room and plopped onto the leather couch while Brian typed at his desk. "Brian, I feel useless. I began working in New York the second week I lived here. I worked multiple jobs and auditioned constantly for theater roles. I worked day and night sometimes. Not working at all is not in my range of understanding. I haven't worked since we arrived June twenty-sixth. I can't wrap my head around it."

Brian walked over and gave me a hug. "Christina, don't worry. It's all going to work out. Have faith and trust God."

I was certain that I did not have the drive or desire to look for theater roles, but I thought I could handle being a tour guide again. Before Brian and I married and moved to Raleigh, I had worked as a tour guide for five years to earn my living while I looked for my big break on Broadway. I began calling my former tour companies, but the news wasn't good.

"We can't take you back, Christina," said Eva, the tour manager at the double-decker office. "There's just no work to be had."

I got similar answers from all my former tour group employers. Who needed to hire tour guides when no tourists were coming to the City?

I scoured the help-wanted ads for backstage tour group leaders and hotel concierge jobs. None were advertised.

"So, how is your job search going, Brian? Any new leads?"

Brian had quit his high-level job at IBM because of me. The

company had transferred him to Raleigh about the time we married, but after a year, I was so unhappy that Brian quit in order to bring me back to New York, the city I loved. He had several promising leads before 9/11, and I assumed he would have new interviews soon.

"I have to admit I'm feeling disjointed," Brian said sheepishly. "I just can't look for work until we're settled back a bit more. If the attacks have hurt the financial sector like I've heard, then I might have to put the search on hold for a bit."

Surprised, I responded, "Okaaaayyyy, but it could be weeks or months before we get some income flowing. What will we do for money?"

"I have savings, and we can cash in stock options. Don't worry, we'll be fine."

I frowned, unconvinced.

"Sweetheart, c'mon, let's think about this a different way," my analytical husband chided me. "It's a blessing we're not employed. That's why we were home together on the morning of 9/11 and how we've been able to be together ever since. Could you imagine having to go straight back to work after the attacks? I'm not sure either of us are up to that now."

I knew he was right, but it still scared me. "Brian, our new home and neighborhood's a mess, we have no jobs, and it seems we're both questioning our careers. Employment prospects are bleak for both of us. I'm an actress and a tour guide and you're in the financial industry—those kinds of jobs don't exist just anywhere, so it's not like we can just move back to Tallahassee and find easy work. Besides, living a year away from the City nearly made me crazy. But using our limited savings doesn't sound fine to me either. Are we at our own Ground Zero?"

"Christina, there is light at the end of this tunnel," he said gently. "I need you to trust that. Trust me. Trust God."

I wanted to trust Brian. And God. I wanted to be as calm as

my husband seemed to be right now. But I was more than a little bit scared. Ever since I moved to New York City at age twenty-three, I had always been prepared with a Plan A, and also a Plan B, C—all the way to Z! But I now found myself at the end of the alphabet and out of letters, adrift and confused. I couldn't quit worrying.

I feel like such a bad person for not trusting God, for not being "a good Christian." I'm worrying instead of praying. But worrying seems natural, and praying takes effort, and I don't have the energy or will-power to fight what is coming naturally right now.

The day after this conversation with Brian, I admitted my worries about money and jobs to Michelle, one of my oldest friends in the City. She reminded me that people all over the world had been donating to charities to help people who had been harmed on 9/11 and encouraged me to seek help from Redeemer Presbyterian Church, where her husband is the music director.

"But we're not poor! And we don't even attend Redeemer," I argued. "I can't just barge in there and ask for money."

"You don't have to attend the church to qualify," Michelle said. "Donors all over the world have sent money to Redeemer to help the people who need it. Christians donated money to this fund for people like you. So get over your pride, and go over there."

Her words hit me like a slap in the face. Was I really being prideful? "I simply don't think we've suffered enough to require assistance," I said. "Thousands of people died that day, thousands more were injured. Brian and I are OK. I can't point to any physical harm we suffered on 9/11. We *can* work. Eventually, we'll get new jobs."

My friend was unmoved. "I repeat," she said stubbornly, "get over your pride, and go over there."

The conversation left me troubled and confused. I had always managed to stay ahead of my bills. All by myself. And now, as an extremely independent thirty-two-year-old, I was not eager to ask for help. I thought I should be capable of overcoming anything with my "I got this!" attitude.

God figured into my life plan, but I still held tightly to the idea that *I* made my successes happen. God was a well-qualified counselor for personal struggles, but I had spent years proving to myself and everyone else that I had it all under control, and I was horrified at the idea that I might need help now. But I couldn't stop thinking about Michelle's comment that people all over the world were donating money for "people like me."

Maybe some of those people who contributed to Redeemer weren't only thinking about surviving relatives of people who died. Maybe a few gave money with people like me and Brian in mind.

Eventually, I talked to Brian about the possibility of asking Redeemer for money.

"No way, Christina! We are not that bad off. We are *fine*. We have been fine and we will be fine. We don't need charity," he replied, offended.

I was sorry for bringing it up. I was afraid that Brian's unemployment was already affecting his self-confidence, and I didn't want him to think I was questioning his ability to provide for his family.

—

I hoped that Brian's words would end the argument in my head, but they didn't. Michelle's reaction to my worries seemed like a validation that both my mental stress and our financial concerns were justified. Something deep inside took hold and trumped my pride.

On Monday, October 1, I tiptoed out of the bedroom while Brian was still asleep. I went to his desk and searched through a stack of receipts and mail.

We have a bunch of expenses, but I don't want to make a spreadsheet of everything we've spent! And anyway, I don't want some church *to get too deep into our financial business. Oh, this is perfect—that $517 vet bill. This is a good example of an expense that was incurred totally due to the attacks. I'll just deal with that one.*

I put the bill in my purse, and called Michelle. "Pray for me! I'm off to Redeemer. But I'm a bit wound up."

"Yay! Proud of you. Just tell them what happened. No reason to get worked up."

"Ya know, this is against Brian's wishes," I told her. "But in this case I'll stick to the mantra, 'It's better to beg for forgiveness than to ask for permission.' I'm not even sure they'll give us money anyway. If I don't get any, then Brian won't ever need to know I asked. If the church does give us some financial help, then maybe he will be happy to have it after all."

I kept talking, barely pausing to breathe. "And anyway, he's not asking for it, I am. He will never even meet these people. How bad could it be to receive a check, sight unseen? Brian insists we're fine with money. But what's wrong with a supplement? He could consider it like a FEMA reimbursement, just from the church instead of the government."

Michelle finally cut in, "Are you trying to reassure yourself or rehearse excuses for Brian?"

"I know, I know. I'm just a bundle of nerves. I gotta go, we'll talk later!"

I've never gone against Brian's wishes in our new marriage. I won't do this again. Just this once. These are strange times right now, and I just need to do what I feel I need to do. Lord, please bless this endeavor!

At Redeemer, a receptionist handed me a form to fill out and then ushered me into an office to speak with two women, Andrea and Honya.

"Please, let's sit down and discuss any needs you have due to 9/11," Andrea said.

Taking a deep breath, I delivered our "9/11 story." I didn't know what criteria Redeemer was using to approve reimbursements, so I included a lot of random details, starting with our move from North Carolina. I described Gaby's ailments. I name-dropped Tom Jennings, Michelle's husband, the Redeemer employee who had told her about the fund. While I rambled, I kept looking for signs that I might be talking too much. But the two women listened intently. I finally ran out of nervous energy.

"So ladies, thanks for seeing me and thank you for considering covering the vet bill. We have other bills, but helping with this one would be a relief." I handed them the vet receipt.

Andrea responded professionally, "Christina, thanks for sharing this with us. Please have a seat in the reception area and we'll get right back with you."

I went out into the hallway to wait.

Five minutes later, Andrea and her assistant opened the door and came into the office lobby. Honya was holding a business-sized envelope, which she offered to me. I took it, feeling very awkward.

"Have a good day," Honya said gently, "and we hope you stay well."

"Thank you, ladies," I responded, and headed for the elevator.

I was the only one on the elevator, so as soon as the doors closed, I opened the envelope. Inside was a handwritten check for $517. I was thrilled to receive funds, thrilled our situation had been deemed worthy of help, and thrilled that the process of asking for help was over. I hoped my experience was typical of people asking for help at this church. The whole thing had been short and noninvasive; they had just asked me a simple question; it had been my choice to elaborate. There was no proselytizing (they didn't even ask whether I was a Christian), no plug for Redeemer attendance, no sympathy overload for our situation, no mention of an intrusive follow-up to see if I had spent their money on the vet bill.

Although I was happy with the results, the morning's events had left me uneasy, and I fidgeted uncomfortably on the subway ride back home. I was loath to talk about 9/11 with anyone anymore, and yet I had shared my very personal story with complete strangers. Talking about what happened put me in an instant funk because I got trapped in the emotions of that day. Moreover, I had asked for money—I had never done that before. That was the kind of fund I contributed to, not took from. And I had no idea how I was going to explain the check to Brian.

Arriving home, I took the coward's way out and simply placed the check at the bottom of his stack of bills and receipts and didn't mention it.

Brian didn't mention the check, nor did his demeanor toward me change. But the next morning, I noticed the stack had disappeared and there was a higher balance in our checking account than I had expected when I took cash out of the ATM that day. About $500 higher.

19

Wandering in a 9/11 Daze

"Brian, why is this dust never-ending?" I was carefully wiping away the daily coating one morning. "I never open the windows and I'm very careful when I go in and out onto the terrace not to let the dust in."

"I think the bulldozers, trucks, and cranes that move wreckage from the Ground Zero pile are kicking it up into the air."

"OK, that gives me an idea, then." I began grabbing washcloths from the bathroom and wetting them in the sink. "I'm going to stuff up every crack. That should stop it," I said, placing the wet washcloths at the bottom of the windows and our terrace doors.

The next morning, we woke to another layer of dust covering everything. As I looked into Brian's frustrated face, I said, "Along with that terrible, sulfuric smell, I guess the dust will be a constant issue." He nodded, looking as defeated as I felt.

When I wasn't trying to clean away the dust that collected on every surface in our apartment, I was collecting facts and stories about the 9/11 attacks and the people who died in them. New information was being released daily, and I immersed myself in it. I learned that:

+ Approximately 200 people jumped to their death.
+ About the same number of people died when they were trapped in elevators.
+ At least 1,100 people survived the initial plane crashes and fought to escape while the towers burned.
+ The South Tower collapsed fifty-six minutes after it was hit

by United Airlines Flight 175—the jet that streaked over our heads that morning.

+ The North Tower collapsed 102 minutes after it was hit by American Airlines Flight 11.

+ A Catholic priest named Father Mychal Judge rushed into the complex when he heard about the attacks. He was praying last rites over those who were dead in the North Tower lobby when debris from the collapsing South Tower killed him and many others. Just before he was killed, he was heard repeatedly praying aloud, "Jesus, please end this right now! God, please end this!"

I began to fixate on the horror and to imagine how I would have felt if I had been in the towers or on one of the planes. I could have been leading a tour group through the World Trade Center that morning like I'd done on many mornings for several years! A few people died having gone that day to the towers on job interviews. Brian could have been interviewing with Cantor Fitzgerald. What would have happened to us then?

"Why are you so upset? At least you're still alive!" This was the second time I'd received an email with these exact same words from an out-of-town friend. As I read it, my face grew hot with anger. "Yeah, well, thanks a lot for the support!" I typed back, pressing "send" too quickly to stop myself. I shut the laptop so hard that I had to reopen it to make sure I had not broken the screen.

It had been less than a month since my world had been turned upside down, and I couldn't figure out how to express my feelings to others. When I talked to friends on the phone, I said way too much, so I began letting the calls go to voicemail and stopped responding to emails. My friends from the City were all struggling in their own ways, and my friends from other places couldn't relate at all. I couldn't talk to my mom because she was already so worried about me.

Brian was talking less and less too, so it was very quiet in the apartment. My husband and I seemed to be locked in separate traumas. We avoided speaking about that day as much as possible. It was too raw, too shocking to analyze. I didn't want to burden him with my inner struggles, and I didn't know how to help him with his. I think he felt the same way about me. I accepted our version of coping, and I loved him even more, if possible, through the experience.

Still, I felt very alone.

Eventually, I began counseling sessions over the phone with Carmela, a Christian counselor in Tallahassee who had done our premarital counseling. When I started my first session, I spoke unemotionally about the attacks, as if I were reading a report. By the end of the session, I was sobbing.

"Carmela, the reality of death came uncomfortably close, and I tell you, heaven and hell seem much more real to me now. Brian and I endured fear and terror in ways I could have never imagined, and it ... just ... really sucks."

Carmela spoke calmly and kindly. "It's clear you're suffering from post-traumatic stress disorder. We need to talk about pills and therapy that will help you recover."

"Carmela, I believe you, but I don't want to undertake some big time-consuming regimen. I still feel like a crybaby. Are you sure this won't go away on its own over time?"

"No," she responded firmly. "You'll have to buckle down and get committed to this. I know you can do it."

I made an appointment with a doctor, who sent me to a psychiatrist, who prescribed Prozac. I was still unsure about relying on medication, but I prayed it would help.

20

A Church and a Job: Mid-October

"How about going to church tomorrow? I'd really love to go, Christina."

"Absolutely." For once, I agreed wholeheartedly with Brian's suggestion. No more excuses.

I feel like I've been pretending in my relationship with God. No more pretending. I want something real. And I don't want to lean on this medication forever. I want to lean on God.

"Which church should we go to?" I asked.

"I'm thinking Redeemer. What do you think?"

I smiled and finally broke the silence on this subject that had lasted almost two weeks. "Because of the check?"

Brian chuckled but said, "No. Not because of the money. I don't feel obligated because of their financial gift. I just feel a connection to the church now."

I was relieved that the Redeemer check had finally been brought up and happy to know Brian wasn't angry about it. And I was glad we were going to attend Redeemer.

"Redeemer made a lasting impression on me. You should have seen the dignified way they treated me. And it's exciting to know that so many people around the world sent donations to help Redeemer serve New Yorkers. That means a lot of people have faith in Redeemer."

On October 14, Brian and I took the subway to Hunter College for Redeemer Presbyterian's worship service. We walked the long aisle of the large college auditorium to sit in the front.

"Gee, it feels like we're about to listen to a college lecture," I whispered to Brian. On the stage was a band, and Tom, Michelle's husband, was seated at the piano. Seeing a familiar face made me feel instantly comfortable.

A vibrant energy filled the slightly worn, secular college auditorium, which was packed with young, smartly dressed professionals. I estimated that there were a couple of thousand people there.

We launched into the traditional hymn "Come Thou Fount of Every Blessing," and I was shocked to hear the band's energetic, upbeat jazz interpretation of the familiar tune. Another jazzed-up hymn followed, then a member of the congregation stepped to the microphone to describe how God had changed his heart through a church program. He was well-spoken and genuine.

Then, a tall, bald gentleman got up to speak. He seemed to be one of the very few people at the church over the age of thirty-five. According to the bulletin, his name was Dr. Timothy Keller. Like the service itself, Dr. Keller was different. He didn't wear a robe. He didn't even use a lectern. A simple music stand slightly off to his side held any notes that weren't in his hand at the moment.

At First Baptist in Tallahassee, our preacher gave emotional sermons filled with charming personal anecdotes and sports analogies. Dr. Keller referenced the *New York Times Magazine* and Karl Marx to emphasize his biblical points. And he talked. Directly to me, it seemed, throughout a three-point, forty-five-minute sermon.

He talked about understanding our personal idols—those things we elevate to the status of God and (often unknowingly) worship. "Sin isn't only doing bad things, it is more fundamentally making good things into ultimate things. Sin is building your life and meaning on anything—even a very good thing— more than on God. Whatever we build our life on will drive us and enslave us. Sin is primarily idolatry."

Hmmmmm … my desire to be a Broadway performer. My love for New York. My quest to be independent. I've made all those "good" things "ultimate" things. My New York City ideals of success were my idols. This totally resonates with me.

After the sermon, the young guy who had led us through the service announced, "The attacks of 9/11 have brought in many newcomers, so we'll be adding a fourth worship service to Redeemer's Sunday schedule."

Brian and I looked at each other knowingly. "I guess we're not the only ones," I said.

When the service was over, Brian and I followed the crowd to a coffee hour located in Hunter's cafeteria. Several hundred people were jockeying for position around a long table with coffee urns and plastic plates stacked high with mini muffins.

I grabbed a handful of flyers, brochures, and leaflets describing the church's programs and services while Brian stood in line for coffee. One flyer advertised socials and Bible studies for performers. A "Classifieds" leaflet advertised apartments that were available, items for sale, professional services, and job opportunities.

One brochure described Redeemer's founding in 1989 and connection to the Presbyterian Church in America. Another described how to become a member. Brian and I enthusiastically agreed to take the first step and attend a class about membership.

"I loved the service today; I really did," Brian told me.

I was glad he agreed. This church already felt like "home" to me.

Thanks for putting Redeemer in our path, Lord! I pray this will be a special church for Brian and me, and that my relationship with you will grow stronger here.

⁓

Back at Le Rivage, I looked through the "Classifieds" leaflet again, and noticed that the Billy Graham Rapid Response Team, a program within the Billy Graham organization based in North

Carolina, needed a receptionist for a disaster relief office it was opening in New York.

I knew I wasn't a strong candidate for a receptionist position, but I needed a job. And I was intrigued by the idea of helping people in the aftermath of 9/11. I convinced myself I could do it.

"This is no time to get picky," I told Brian. "We need the money. I think I should at least apply."

I was able to line up an interview that same week and was surprised to find only a few other applicants there. I learned that the organization planned to focus on counseling for those who were affected by the attacks. At the end of the interview, John said, "I think you might be a good fit for this job. We'd like for you to consider joining us. You could start October 22 as a full-time employee."

"Thank you so much," I said, trying not to act too excited outwardly. Inwardly I was cheering.

21

Queen of a War Zone

THE WEEKEND BEFORE I WAS SUPPOSED to start my new job, I took a long look at myself in the bathroom mirror. It had been a long time since I had tried to look presentable—any efforts that hinted of vanity had felt unseemly after 9/11. But that day I realized that there is a difference between vanity and self-respect, so I gave myself a facial and colored my own hair for the first time ever. On Monday, I woke up two hours early so I had plenty of time to dress and apply my makeup.

After a substantial amount of time and effort, I felt my appearance was somewhat back to normal. The rest of me—well, that was a work in progress. I took an antidepressant before I left the apartment. So far the medicine was making me feeling better—calmer, less depressed, and perkier. However, I was being cautious in emailing or phoning family and friends; I didn't want to get upset or worked up. I didn't trust myself or these pills just yet.

Lord, please let me do well today. Please give me strength and confidence that I can do this. Let me be a blessing to this organization and the people they'll be serving.

John welcomed me when I arrived at the compact Chelsea office, showing me around and introducing me to the rest of the staff. All eight were licensed counselors from North Carolina who had worked in similar roles after the Oklahoma City bombing in 1995. He walked me to my desk. "It's a pretty standard office job," he said. "Answer phone calls, take messages, and generally help with small tasks."

I sat at my desk and read information about the organization.

After a few hours, the phone rang. "Billy Graham organization, may I help you?" I said as professionally as I could muster.

"Hi, I'm here in Alabama, and I want to know: is there anything I can do to help? What does everyone need up there?"

I answered, "Thank you, I'm not sure at this point. Can I take down your name and number?"

I got several similar calls during the day. Late in the afternoon, an older woman called and asked, "Honey, can you give me any prayer requests so I can pray for you all?" That call melted my heart.

I asked John what I should do with the calls from people who wanted to come to the City to help. He handed me a list of local nonprofit organizations. "Suggest they contact one of them," he told me. "We focus mainly on counseling at this office, and we just aren't set up to accept and utilize volunteers."

When I got home that evening, I told Brian, "The setting is different than I expected; it's all business. The atmosphere is professional and reserved. But the job is gonna be a piece of cake! I only answered about ten calls. It's a sleepy little office. This'll be easy!"

The next day, John said, "There's another task that we need you to do daily—organizing materials." He took me to a room filled with boxes. "People have been sending donations from all over the world to distribute to 9/11 victims. We need to sort them so we know what to do with them."

"Sounds great," I said, as I began opening the boxes. The first was filled with dozens of toys and the next with books about Jesus. Several others held hundreds of Bibles. I sorted, tagged, and counted everything.

When 5:00 came, I walked to the subway, eager to get home to Brian. I was dismayed when the train stopped at Canal Street, far short of my planned destination, "due to disruptions from the World Trade Center attacks." I walked the extra mile and wearily trudged into our apartment.

"I had to walk home again, Brian. The subway lines that are still running are so spotty! Looks like I'm going to have to factor in a surprise hike home, after having paid for a full ride. This is going to get old real quick."

A week went by, and I settled into the office environment but found that I had little contact with the other employees, who were always busy in their cubicles. Secretly, I had been hoping that I could find a way to talk to one of the counselors about my own 9/11 experiences, but I never found a good opportunity to approach one of them. I was afraid it would be seen as a conflict of interest to be working for a relief organization and getting free services at the same time.

So I kept quiet and didn't tell anyone there "my story."

The well-intentioned, but often clueless, calls continued. A Midwestern youth pastor told me, "I want to send a youth mission trip to help in the 9/11 aftermath. Could you help find us a service project to engage in?" I was glad the caller couldn't see me rolling my eyes as I pictured teens from some rural town feverishly sweeping the never-ending yellow dust off Manhattan streets.

The most exciting part of my day occurred every afternoon when the donation packages arrived. Organizing the items had become my daily entertainment, and I would dive into the boxes with gusto.

One afternoon, I opened a box of what appeared to be Rubik's cubes. But the cube's typical bright colors had been replaced by pictures of Jesus, crosses, and other spiritual scenes. Instead of matching the colored squares, you were supposed to put the picture of Jesus back together. It was called the "Evangacube." I was baffled—and somewhat offended.

Who's supposed to play with these right now? Someone who lost a job, someone forced out of their home? I can't imagine going to the home of someone who experienced a loss and saying, "Sorry about your loss.

Here's an Evangacube."

Next came a box filled with small tins of packaged mints called "Testamints."

That has GOT to be a joke.

The next several boxes were filled with teddy bears with personal notes attached to each of them.

This is so sweet and well-meaning—someone spent a lot of time on those notes. But in my opinion they're unnecessary and impossible to distribute.

I told Brian about the shipments that night.

"How do you get teddy bears to the kids who were affected by 9/11? These local children have families, most likely wealthy ones. And they're all scattered now to different schools, and many have moved out of the area.

"And people are sending boxes and boxes of Bibles. But this is New York City. If you're a Christian, you already have a Bible. If you're not, you are not looking for a Bible."

Brian agreed but asked, "Are New Yorkers coming to the office? They might be searching for God in this time of crisis."

"The office is open to walk-ins and people who called to schedule counseling appointments. But very few people are coming in. The few that do walk in are looking for ways to volunteer—just like most of my callers."

Brian delved further. "What do you think about the assistance the organzation is providing? Do you believe in what they're doing?"

I thought deeply before I responded. "I see a culture clash. I understand what my well-meaning colleagues are trying to accomplish. They have the best intentions ever. But I also feel and see what the City is going through and how New Yorkers respond to charity—both at this office and in all the donation depots I visited.

"New Yorkers are a tough, skeptical bunch. Even a native

would find it difficult to meet these victims' needs. I can't help but compare what's going on in my office to how Redeemer is helping people. That church is reaching New Yorkers in a way that impacts their physical and spiritual well-being. Redeemer helped us with our practical needs, which ultimately drew us to want to attend their church."

The longer I worked for the Billy Graham Rapid Response Team, the harder it became to work in an office created for 9/11 victims when I couldn't tell anyone that I was also a victim. It was hard for me to watch idle counselors who had no clients to help. And hard for me to watch clients come in to talk to the counselors. I wanted to both get help and help others, but I had a hard time talking about my experience with anyone. I wanted counseling but couldn't ask for it. My frustration turned to resentment, and I'm sure my bad attitude was evident to those in the office.

On the Friday evening of my third week at work, I took the subway home, as usual, sitting numb and exhausted as the train crawled down the tracks. Once again, without warning, train service abruptly ended at Canal Street. The tears started as I climbed up the subway steps. At home, I tried to "medicate" myself by sipping a big glass of wine and reading a good book instead of turning on the TV. Brian turned in early while I continued reading.

At midnight, I looked up from my book and glanced out the windows toward the huge spotlights that lit Ground Zero, allowing the clean-up of "the pile" to go on twenty-four hours a day. I set my glass down, got up, threw a blanket around me, and stepped out into the chilly night. I closed my eyes and tried to imagine the view as it used to be.

I remembered standing on the terrace and practicing my "Queen Elizabeth wave" shortly after we moved into this apartment. I had felt like royalty as I gazed across at the thousands of lights shining from residences, offices, streetlights, head-lights, and boats sailing lazily down the Hudson. But the real stars of the show were the Twin Towers, which resembled lit-up Christmas trees at night. I would lie on our terrace lawn chairs and just stare at them for hours, dazzled. Clearly, God had delivered me from my hardscrabble earlier years in New York and brought me back to the city I loved. I was certain that I stood at the edge of a bright future as a new wife and future Broadway star.

Opening my eyes, I saw deformed shapes of debris that had replaced the twinkling lights. Particles of dust in the air shone like reflections on shattered glass. The Ground Zero spotlights cast ghostly shadows. And where the twin towers used to be, just a dark, lonely expanse. Only two months ago, I had felt like a queen standing on that terrace. Now I felt like the queen of a war zone.

Unexpectedly, I thought of the cross-stitched words that had hung in my childhood bedroom in Tallahassee: "There's a simple truth so very plain to see. Whatever I become, is simply up to me." Those words had served as my mantra during the years I fought to turn my adolescent dreams of New York City stardom into reality. I shook my head bitterly as they rose unbidden in my mind.

Nope. It's not up to me. All this wasn't "up to me." The people in the planes and towers—what became of them wasn't "up to them." I don't believe that little motto anymore.

Feeling the sadness of broken dreams, I stepped back inside, closing the terrace doors tightly behind me. The dreams that made me fall in love with the apartment were now the nightmares that haunted me. Antidepressants could not blind me to the wreckage outside my window or ease the delays and frustrations I experienced every time I left my home or wipe away the dust I woke up to each morning.

The terrors we experienced on 9/11 and the hardships we had

faced since that day had stripped me down and left me bare of all the things I had counted on for most of my life. What was left was either gonna make me or break me. I leaned against the terrace door in prayer.

Lord, I need you. I need YOU. I don't want all the good things you've given me—my husband, my talents, my work ethic, my love for this City—to be ultimate things that are above you. I want you. "Whatever I become" is simply up to YOU now.

22

Home for the Holidays

THE NEXT MONDAY, NOVEMBER 12, I quit the Billy Graham job. Working with 9/11 victims had sounded like a good idea when I applied for the job, but in reality that was the last thing I should have been doing. The job kept me oversaturated in the trauma. Stepping away, I finally started to see how spiritually sidelined I had been and how physically exhausted I was.

On the same day I quit, only sixty-two days after 9/11, American Airline Flight 587, en route from New York to the Dominican Republic, crashed into a neighborhood in Belle Harbor, Queens, killing 265 people. It was one of the deadliest aviation accidents ever to occur on US soil.

"They're saying it's not terrorism!" I was ranting to Brian. "I have a hard time believing that. It happened on November *twelfth* and in New York City! Can that be a coincidence?" The crash had rattled nerves across the country but especially in the City. Although it would later be proven that terrorists played no part in it, the loss of so many lives just added to the grief and trauma.

Brian acknowledged my fears and then said, "Christina, I have some more bad news. I saw this on the news this morning. They are finally beginning to understand what materials the dust is made up of. The grey-yellow dust that hit us was a mixture of pulverized plaster and crumpled concrete, with crushed wood and wire. And human remains."

I could think of nothing to say. After a few minutes, I started in on a speech I had been rehearsing since Friday.

"Honey, I've fought the good fight here. I tried. I did my best.

But the living situation in downtown Manhattan isn't going to change soon. It all seems like too much to tackle right now. I want rest, I want peace. I think it's time to go. Can we just—get out of here? Can we just leave? We could head to Florida, stay with our moms, decompress for a while."

I had been afraid to look at Brian while I talked and so was surprised when he answered quickly. "Sure we can. Getting out of town sounds kinda great."

He agreed so quickly that I wondered if God had been nudging him toward the same conclusion.

⁓

We spent the day packing, preparing to stay away at least until after New Year's. Apart from spending Christmas in Florida, we had no detailed plans, but I was not bothered by the uncertainty. In fact, I was thrilled at the prospect of not seeing devastation every time I looked out the window.

"We'll have a car. A car! What a luxury!" I was almost giddy with excitement.

On Tuesday, Brian picked up a rental car, and we loaded it quickly. Gaby hopped in with excitement that I had not seen in weeks—he must have felt our own emotions. Exiting the Holland Tunnel, I felt as if a huge burden had been lifted off my chest. I opened the car window and breathed deeply; the air was so fresh! I couldn't help but think about the day we had returned to New York City from Raleigh just four months ago. I had been bouncing on the seat singing "New York, New York"! I wasn't singing today, but I was just as excited to be getting the heck out of that place.

But my excitement began giving way to anxiety even before we got off the New Jersey Turnpike. I began to wonder what kind of reception we would receive in other parts of the country. After all, it was my out-of-town friends who kept telling me I was overreacting.

"I'm excited to see my mom and visit friends in my hometown, but I don't think I'm ready to go to barbecues and parties and act like everything's OK," I told Brian.

"Is that what people are doing around the States nowadays?"

"I guess so. I'm just assuming that the rest of the country has moved on with daily life. New York City has always been practically its own planet. I think the attacks have pushed it even further away."

I also regretted leaving Redeemer just as we were getting settled there. "We were really trying to blaze a path there, and now we're blazing out just as fast. Brian, do you think it will be possible to pick up right where we left off when we return to New York?"

Brian tried to reassure me, but my anxieties were bubbling over.

Eventually, I reached the source of my fountain of worry. "I'm happy to leave, but I feel like a traitor," I told Brian. "We're abandoning New York. We're taking the easy way out. I won't be giving out teddy bears. I won't be helping to rebuild. I can't even hold a job as a receptionist. I feel guilty leaving when I know so many people can't get away."

Brian cut me off—sharply this time. "Stop it, don't go there. You have *got* to get out of the City, and you know it. No one 'needs' you right now. New York will carry on without you. Focus on the good, Christina. God is making it very clear we need a change of scenery!"

He took my hand, and my anxieties began to recede.

I convinced Brian to take a detour to Gatlinburg, Tennessee, where we checked into a tiny cabin and spent the afternoon hiking in the Smoky Mountain National Park. I drank in the beautiful woods and scent of pine in complete silence as twilight crept in. Although I tried to focus on the joy I felt being surrounded by nature, I began to feel confused and disoriented. I simply could not stop thinking about the City or the past two months. Even in the middle of a forest, I didn't feel completely safe.

Birds chirping outside our windows woke me the next morning. It was a wonderful reminder that we were no longer in New York. We drove into town for breakfast and then headed for the charming tourist shops on Main Street.

"Wow, Brian, look at the flags!"

From one end of Main Street to the other, American flags were flying in shop after shop, along with red, white, and blue ribbons and decorations of every kind. Banners and posters paying tribute to those who died, especially New York City firefighters and police officers, were hanging in windows and door frames of shops and restaurants. As we popped in and out of souvenir shops, I was astonished to see that each and every one carried a vast array of items related to 9/11. T-shirts carried pictures of the Twin Towers before and after the attacks. Shirts and caps sported slogans such as "America Is #1," "Never Forget," and "Don't Mess with the US." There were framed prints of prayers for the deceased, and posters that declared calls to war. Christian crosses and fish symbols were featured on many of the collectibles. Gatlinburg was one big 9/11 tribute.

"So this is it," I said, showing Brian a T-shirt with the image of the Twin Towers. "This is how the rest of America is reacting to 9/11. Everyone else is just as upset as we are. I had no idea."

"I'm almost relieved," Brian replied, surveying the shirts and signs around the store.

"Yes, the tributes are in the form of tacky Gatlinburg souvenirs and T-shirts, but the town is filled with them! And people are wearing them! They care. Brian, if these tributes are all over Gatlinburg," I reasoned, "then 9/11 is still on everyone's hearts. The rest of the country hasn't forgotten us!"

Based on some unhelpful emails and phone calls, I had wondered if New Yorkers had been abandoned by the rest of the country. I worried word wasn't getting out, that people didn't know how bad the attacks had been or how much damage they had done to the City. But it wasn't true. It wasn't "New Yorkers" and "the rest of America," as I feared. People far from Manhattan were grieving and angry too.

I was surprised that some T-shirts in a souvenir store could make me feel less alone.

As we continued to drive down rural roads through Tennessee and Georgia, I saw many 9/11-related flags, posters, and signs fluttering from farmhouses, barns, houses, and storefronts. Patriotic billboards declared "Never Forget" in almost every county. American flags were flying from barns and front porches and even tractors.

My worries about being isolated when I left New York melted into pure exhilaration.

23

Healing from Home

WE PULLED INTO MOM'S DRIVEWAY one night a few days after we had left New York. I bounded out of the car, and Mom took me in her arms and said, "I'm sooo happy to see you two." She let go long enough to ask, "What took you so long?" Then she gave me another hug—the longest one I ever remembered from her.

Mom still lives in the house where I grew up, an A-frame farmhouse with rocking chairs on the big front porch, where I headed after unpacking a little. The house is set back into the woods, surrounded by tall trees. In the moonlight, I lounged in the cozy hammock in our large backyard near a white gazebo. I wandered back inside, finding deep comfort in all my mom's cherished trinkets and heirlooms—antiques passed down from my great-grandmother, china pieces hand-painted by my grandmother, the shelf of my dusty pageant trophies and crowns, framed family portraits from bygone days. I especially treasured the pictures of me and my dad, who had died shortly after I graduated from college.

On my first morning in Tallahassee I woke after a good night's sleep—one of the best I'd had in a while—and pulled up the blinds. Instead of a gaping hole and charred metal, I saw green grass, tall trees, and flowers. As I walked through the living room, I saw no dust on Mom's furniture. I made a cup of coffee and took it to the front porch to enjoy from the hanging swing. I breathed in the fresh air, picked up the *Tallahassee Democrat* from the porch, and happily read about the local winter festival and annual holiday charity drive.

Later, Brian and I headed to the nearby Meridian Park, so Gaby could roam its woodsy trails. Doing some errands around town, I was grateful to see no military officers in combat gear stationed at Governor's Square Mall. Local fire and police stations were not draped in mourning buntings or memorial flowers. In Gatlinburg, I had been relieved to find signs that people outside of New York City had also been deeply affected by the September 11 attacks. In Tallahassee, I was relieved to find that life looked much the same as it had on September 10. The people of Tallahassee were clearly mourning the terrorist attacks and loss of life, but 9/11 did not dominate every aspect of their daily lives.

I made it my goal to achieve that two-sided coin of remembrance—to be able to move forward with my life while never forgetting the devastation and the ones who had been lost. And Tallahassee provided the perfect place for me to work toward that goal. Every day I felt more relaxed. The heaviness that had been my constant companion for two months seemed to lift a little more every day. Light was beginning to penetrate my darkness. I could even go a few hours without thinking about 9/11 and New York City.

I found extra solace back at First Baptist Church, where I soaked up the new pastor's sermon on gratitude. Somehow, word spread that "Chrissy Ray from New York" was in the building, and old friends and acquaintances approached from every corner, bringing hugs and handshakes and words of heartfelt concern and encouragement.

Although some of the questions and remarks were naive, I felt none of my earlier irritability about the clueless comments. Nor did I feel compelled to unload stream-of-consciousness descriptions about everything I had experienced. Many of the older people didn't seem to make the New York connection and greeted me just like they had since I was a kid. Those greetings were especially refreshing, making life feel normal for just a moment. Seeing those familiar and friendly faces rejuvenated me.

Brian got as much love and attention as I did, even though most of my hometown church knew him only from our wedding there twenty months earlier. The look on Brian's face told me he loved the warm welcome as much as I did, which thrilled me. I wanted him to find strength in all these wonderful good wishes just as I was. As I watched Brian shake hands with my lifelong friends, I thought that his even-keeled temperament had helped him escape my wild ride on the emotional roller coaster. He had long since quit sleeping throughout the day and seemed mostly back to his old self.

Being in Tallahassee meant I was able to see Carmela in face-to-face counseling sessions, which I counted as one of the many blessings of our trip. In our first meeting, I told Carmela about my activities, reactions, and feelings directly after the attacks up until when we arrived in Tallahassee. I also mentioned Brian and how we had avoided discussing the events of that day.

"So what do you think, Carmela? Was I having a nervous breakdown or something? What's been happening to us?"

Carmela reassured me, saying, "The irritability and anger, withdrawal from others, the difficulty sleeping and nightmares— they're all symptoms of post-traumatic stress disorder. I haven't talked to Brian, but I suspect he is suffering from it, too. The avoidance of discussion is a strong indicator of PTSD. By the way, I read recently that twenty percent of people living within a one-mile radius of the Twin Towers are suffering from post-traumatic stress disorder. Did you know that?"

"No, I didn't," I said, stunned. "Do you really think we have PTSD? I thought that was for soldiers after horrific battles."

"Yes. It's pretty evident. My advice is that you don't try pressuring Brian into talking. It's often very difficult for people with

PTSD to talk about their trauma, and it can even make things worse for some people. Never try to force Brian to open up. Comfort often comes from your companionship and acceptance, rather than from talking."

Leaning in, toward me, Carmela continued, "The attacks of 9/11 threw a wrench in your worldview and sense of safety. It tore the fabric of your daily lives. It's not like you witnessed a traumatic event in another country. It's where you live. It's where you go shopping and walk your dog and take tourist groups. Places you see every day. Your mind is having a hard time accepting. You probably decided to come to Tallahassee because your mind wanted to attempt to restore your sense of order."

It all made so much sense. "OK, what about the obsession with the news? The endless walking?"

She answered, "The constant news-watching is probably related to your reason for coming back to Tallahassee. You subconsciously thought reading and digesting information would help you understand the events more, which in turn might restore your sense of order. Your walking around town allowed you to commune with people and get helped by volunteers at charity places—that is both a cathartic coping mechanism and an emotional outlet. Being around volunteers and fellow mourners also helped restore your worldview. You've always believed the world to be good, but the attacks brought that fundamental belief into question. Being around people who wanted to help others reassured you that the world is not all evil.

"Plus, it's very healing and comforting to be around people. Opportunities to be constructive and productive help people who are under duress. You thought going to retrieve items gave you purpose, which is something you needed after the attacks. Plus, honestly, the attacks probably did put you into some manic episodes and fight-or-flight responses, which accounts for the incessant walking."

"So what do I do now?" It was nice to hear rationales for some of my behaviors, but I also wanted to know how to move forward.

"I definitely think you should continue with antidepressants, and keep reading books as a relaxation technique rather than watching the news. Believe it or not, you should continue walking, or at least exercising. Exercise releases endorphins and improves your mood and outlook. And no drinking or smoking! That kind of self-medication is no good for you."

I winced at that suggestion, as I had been increasingly indulging in both.

"Being around people is good for you," Carmela told me. "People you trust. And be patient with people in general—they're not out to get you. Also be patient with *yourself.* This will all take some time."

I left her office a little lighter and eager for our next meeting. Each time I met with Carmela, I felt like a load of bricks had been lifted from my back.

I was surprised by Carmela's suggestion that Brian was also suffering from PTSD. He seemed like such a rock these days. But in early December, an incident involving Gaby made me realize that Brian was not back to normal either. Gaby was clearly feeling the best he had since 9/11; he wasn't wheezing, throwing up, or pawing at his eyes and his face had been fixed in a perpetual dog-smile ever since we had left the City. He loved being in Mom's backyard, and I loved being able to just let him outside rather than leashing him up and pacing concrete streets.

One morning, I let Gaby out into the backyard and watched from the window for a few minutes as he happily rolled around in the sweetgrass. About an hour later, I opened the door and called for him. No response. I walked out and began searching the half-acre backyard, yelling Gaby's name. When I got to the fence, I realized there were plenty of places Gaby could squeeze underneath, and I knew he had escaped.

I ran inside. "Brian, Mom, Gaby's gone. He's run away. We have to find him!"

Brian looked as if I had just slapped him. He appeared pale and crestfallen and offered no ideas about searching for our dog, so I took charge, driving around the neighborhood with my friend Cindy. After a fruitless search, we returned to the house to make posters we could hang around the area. As Cindy looked for markers and poster board, I looked for Brian and found him sound asleep in our bed. It was 3:00 in the afternoon.

Cindy, Mom, and I made "Missing Boston Terrier" posters, and I spent the rest of the afternoon driving around the area, hanging signs and checking the ditches on both sides of the road. I looked for Gaby until the sun went down. I didn't see Brian leave my childhood bedroom for the rest of the day.

The next morning we got a call from a man who had seen our signs. He had spotted Gaby running back and forth across a busy thoroughfare the day before, coaxed him into his car to keep him safe from traffic, and took him to his home, which was less than a mile away.

"Gaby's been found!" I yelled in the direction of the bedroom where Brian was still sleeping. It only took a few minutes to collect our wandering dog and return to Mom's house. "We're back," I yelled, thinking Brian would be ecstatic to see us.

Instead, he strolled casually into the living room. Gaby ran to Brian, jumping on him and licking his face. Brian gave Gaby a hug and then went back to the bedroom and went back to sleep. For the next few days, Brian slept more than he was awake, just like he had after 9/11.

The next time I saw Carmela, I told her she had been right about Brian. He was still suffering too.

24

A Different Kind of Holiday

As much as I was enjoying being in Florida, I did not want to lose sight of what was happening in the City. I called Sarah and Michelle constantly, treating my girlfriends like reporters who could give me the inside scoop on all things New York. Their updates helped me feel connected to the City I still cherished and thought about constantly.

"Michelle, what's going on in the City now? Anything up with Redeemer?"

"Redeemer is still bursting at the seams. It has grown from 2,800 to 5,400 since the attacks. I heard forty percent more people are attending religious services now in the City in general. Oh, and you'll love this—I've been volunteering at a soup kitchen in Hell's Kitchen, and a ton of volunteers show up there every Saturday. Yep, New Yorkers are still feeling way altruistic. I feel like it's a complete *culture* shift that we're witnessing."

Sarah gave me updates on the Broadway scene, which was still suffering but showing some encouraging signs. I learned that the City had bought 50,000 Broadway tickets to give to charities and rescue workers, which helped boost morale and the shows themselves.

I also kept watching the news, although not as obsessively as I had earlier. I still wanted to know as much as possible about the recovery of the City and also the progress of the military action in Afghanistan that had started shortly after 9/11. Operation Enduring Freedom generated a lot of conflicting opinions in the country—and even in my own family.

Mom, a pacifist, didn't agree with the war but was also upset by ongoing threats of terror, including anthrax letters that had been discovered in multiple places. "I pray this craziness dies down soon so people can start getting back to their lives and not be a slave to fear!"

"Getting back to normal isn't going to happen anytime soon, Mom," I said. "Not when human remains are being discovered and identified daily. Fires still haven't been put out where the towers fell. For people like Brian and me, it feels like the attacks just happened yesterday!"

Then I went a step further to broach a subject I had been thinking about a lot lately. "I don't know how the country is gonna pull off Christmas this year."

I returned to the subject a few days later. "Mom, it's been such a hard year. In addition to the 9/11 attacks, this will be the first Christmas without your dad, who died in March. And Brian's dad died in July. He doesn't talk about it much, but I know that he misses him and that the holidays will be especially hard. Maybe we shouldn't celebrate Christmas at all."

Mom shot me a horrified look. "You can't be serious!" Christmas was always celebrated to the fullest in my house. Not celebrating would be incomprehensible to my mother.

"I don't really mean not celebrate at all, Mom." I quickly retreated, not wanting to upset her. "But I can tell you right now that I'm not up for all of the things I usually enjoy doing at Christmastime. Decorating trees, caroling, and watching all the Christmas specials—I just can't bring myself to participate in all that. Gifts and parties seem inappropriate and downright disrespectful now."

So, we compromised. Mom put up all her usual decorations, but she didn't ask Brian or me to participate in all of the parties or the usual festivities. But we were happy to fulfill our Christmas Eve tradition of attending First Baptist's special candlelight service.

"This year, humanity and our planet felt more fragile and finite," the pastor preached. "Really, the message of Christmas is more important than ever. We need to reimagine how to celebrate it this year." That caught my attention. Then he discussed the familiar account of angels who told startled shepherds to "fear not." That resonated with me too.

I've seen other-worldly, fantastical sights this year, and I understand fear now in a way I didn't before. I understand why God didn't want the shepherds to fear—and I understand that he doesn't want me to fear death, or supernatural sights, or the future. Those are the things I've been afraid of lately. But I'm starting to realize that I had a lot of fear even before the attacks happened. I feared others' judgments and opinions of me. I feared I wouldn't succeed. God doesn't want me to fear those things either. He wants me to know and sense his sovereignty in all things.

"Matthew 1:23 says that Jesus would be called Emmanuel, 'God with us,' and he would save people from their sins," the pastor continued.

This means God is with me, he is literally with me always. He was with me when we evacuated 21 West. He was with me as we were running around Battery Park while the towers were coming down. And saving people from their sins in my case often means saving me from myself. My self-condemnation is epic. When I fail to accomplish something, I tear myself apart and go into a shame spiral. That's because I've been relying on myself. When I rely on myself, I think my failures are all my fault and my successes are all by my own strength.

Everything I had struggled with in my life seemed to be interconnected. I could see I needed to let go, put God in control, and trust in his plans.

The sermon ended with a verse from Revelation: "He will wipe away every tear from their eyes. There will be no more death or mourning or crying or pain, for the old order of things has passed away."

The new order is on its way. Well, Praise the Lord for that, because from what I exerienced this year, the old order stinks!

After Christmas we traveled to Melbourne, Florida, to visit with Brian's family and celebrate the New Year with them. I was not enthusiastic when my brother-in-law suggested watching the traditional Times Square New Year's Eve party. New Year's Eve isn't a time I tend to celebrate at all, and I've always thought the craziness in Times Square was a bit vulgar.

But when Joe turned the channel to ABC, I was intrigued to see news anchor Peter Jennings hosting a "meaningful and reflective" piece on New Year's celebrations from around the world. "The famous ball that drops in Times Square is special this year," Jennings told us. "It's made of Waterford crystal and is a tribute to those who died on 9/11. It's engraved with the names of the countries and regions that lost citizens—the World Trade Center, the Pentagon, the four airline flights—and the names of uniformed rescue organizations that lost members."

At midnight, we watched this special ball drop in Times Square on TV and yelled "Happy New Year" at the top of our lungs. It was the first New Year's Eve celebration I had ever cared about. I was glad to celebrate the end of 2001.

The next day, Brian wanted to discuss our future.

"What do you think? After a month and a half in Florida, is it time to go home? Is it time to go back to New York? I've prayed about it, and now seems like the right time."

"Yes," I replied. "I feel the same way."

The decision was made just like that—just as quickly and simply as we had made our decision to leave the City and head for Florida.

Some of our friends and family had been urging us to stay in the South, pointing out that we didn't have jobs in the City, so now would be the perfect time to start over elsewhere. But I never felt that was really an option. New York City was my home—the time in Raleigh had made that abundantly plain. Even though the City had changed, it was still the place I felt most comfortable in this world, and I just couldn't see myself living elsewhere. I was so glad to know Brian felt like I did.

Before we left, I said a prayer: *Lord, the book of Jeremiah says, "For I know the plans I have for you," declares the Lord, "plans to prosper you and not to harm you, plans to give you hope and a future." I'm claiming this promise, Lord. Please reveal your plans to us!*

25

Signs of Healing:
January 2002

ON JANUARY 3, 2002, WE BEGAN the eighteen-hour trip north.

We drove mostly in silence for a few hours, until I asked, "Do you realize we're returning to New York City for the second time in five months?"

"Yes, I do," Brian said quietly, keeping his eyes on the road.

I reminisced saying, "Remember me singing 'New York, New York' when we pulled into town? That seems forever ago. We were all about success and the goals we wanted to achieve back then. What about now? What would you say is our purpose?"

"I don't know about you," Brian responded, "but I've got no particular plan or agenda. I just want to see what God has in store for us."

"Me too!" I exclaimed, happy and relieved to know we were on the same page.

How foolish and naive I was last summer. I thought I was leaving behind a tough adjustment period—where I felt like a fish out of water. In fact, any dilemmas I'd experienced before were just preparing me for the hell that was to come. I wasn't emerging from a Ground Zero at that time, I was being prepared for it.

The "January Brian and Christina" were quite different from the "July Brian and Christina." In July, we could foresee an incredible climb to success that would include parties, concerts, shows, fancy restaurants, money. The years of audition frustration, multiple day jobs, and cockroach-infested New York City hovels were behind me. The exile to Raleigh was complete. I was headed back to a city I loved with a man I loved; with his support, I was certain that I would quickly kick-start my lapsed Broadway career. Brian had been sure he would soon land a job with a top financial firm and work his way up the ladder to a comfortable position. In January, we knew only that we were returning to our Financial District apartment. We planned to look for new jobs, get established at Redeemer, and try to find an equilibrium in our "new normal." Beyond that, we were a blank slate.

Although I felt we had changed so much since July, what hadn't changed was the affection and devotion I felt for New York. I still carried that torch from when I fell in love with the City at seventeen while visiting with my high school chorus group. Running even deeper than my love for the City, however, was a deep belief that God had a purpose for me individually—and Brian and me as a couple—in this particular environment. Now, however, I understood in ways that I never had before that I had no control over anything. My career, my home, our finances, our future—I needed to rely on God to provide these things.

"God can turn everything to the good, Brian. We may have some scars, but maybe those scars can be turned into some seriously cool tattoos that could be of use to glorify God."

"Yes, he'll work it all together for his purpose. I believe it too!" Both of us smiled contentedly.

Our declarations of faith did not mean that we had "moved on" from 9/11. Evidence of the attacks was always there. The stress and fear we had felt since that day were also there, an undercurrent, a constant background noise. Maybe it would be there for the rest of our lives. If so, it would exist beside a new understanding of what it means to truly rely on God.

~

Rounding a bend on the New Jersey Turnpike, we caught our first glimpse of Manhattan in the distance. "There it is! Here we come!" I said aloud, admiring that beloved, beautiful skyline.

My eyes were drawn to the cluster of Downtown skyscrap-
ers. The missing towers from that cluster were still a shock to the
senses, but there was no smoke or fire obscuring the view today.
Driving down the West Side Highway, we saw less debris and
dust and more open streets in our neighborhood.

Brian pulled up to our building, and we unloaded our suit-
cases and two air cleaners Mom had purchased for us. I headed
inside while Brian drove off to return the rental car. There were
at least ten people milling around in the lobby, checking their
mail, talking with Flo, and bringing in groceries from the bodega
next door. It was the most people I had seen in the lobby since
September 10.

When I got to our apartment, I headed straight for the terrace.
I walked to the left-hand corner to take in our western view. The
Battery Park City area that had been turned into a "large-debris
trash can" was clear. The crushed fire trucks and other hunks of
debris had been replaced by brown dirt, apparently in prepara-
tion for landscaping.

Debris had also been removed from the open-air parking
garage straight below us. Just north, at Ground Zero, "the pile"
remained, a small mountain of debris. But it was a smaller mountain than when we had left, and it no longer included the fifty-foot
piece of iron facade that had stood upright in the middle. Without
that iconic piece of debris, Ground Zero looked different, more
like a construction site than an open wound.

Back inside, Gaby at my heels, I inspected each room of our
apartment. All looked fine—apart from the ever-present layers
of fine dust. I leashed up Gaby for a potty run, and we were both
delighted to discover that the National Guard was gone from
Battery Park so that we could resume our walks there.

Curious to see the rest of the neighborhood, I walked with
Gaby up to Saint Paul's Chapel via Broadway. Looking at the faces

of the people we passed, I was happy to note that few seemed as glum as they had when we left in the fall. It was the end of the workday, and people were rushing to the subways and waiting in long lines for the buses. Drivers were honking obnoxiously. The general rhythm of the City seemed to have returned.

Saint Paul's was still a major 9/11 memorial, its gate laden with mementos, flags, origami, and stuffed animals. The Deutsche Bank building was still covered in netting. However, a temporary wooden facade the exact height and width of the building had been erected to cover the netting and scaffolding underneath it. A colorful image had been painted on the facade, and since the building was 517 feet with thirty-nine floors, the picture was enormous. It was an American flag in a heart shape with a quote painted underneath: "The human spirit is not measured by the size of the act but by the size of the heart."

That's beautiful, but I'm still hearing that the building is full of toxins and it's releasing them into the neighborhood. Soooo, why the heck are they spending the time to beautify rather than take it down?

As Gaby and I turned toward home, I realized that the toxins and dust would be a constant concern. What effect would all these particles have on us? I sighed and tried to shake off the worries.

We've made our decision. We're here to stay. This is it, this is home. It's time to get moving on our new life, no looking back.

26

Redeemer to the Rescue—Again: February, March 2002

THE CITY WAS RETURNING to a sense of normalcy, and Brian and I needed to as well. It was time for both of us to begin seriously searching for jobs, so Brian began scheduling appointments with headhunters to search for sales, marketing, or finance positions. I reached out to tour companies but was again told that tourism was slow, even for January and February, which are some of the slowest months of the year anyway.

I decided to temp to earn some money and began working as a receptionist, receiving a new assignment each weekday with various companies throughout Manhattan. After three weeks I was already tired of schlepping all over Manhattan during the coldest, snowiest months of the year and so picked up Redeemer's classified ads after church on February 17.

One listing in particular caught my eye: an administrative assistant position for the Redeemer Church Planting Center, the "international arm" of Redeemer. With a little research, I learned that RCPC was founded by Redeemer Presbyterian Church as part of an effort to renew global cities through the planting of gospel-centered churches. "Working in targeted cities in the United States and around the world, RCPC serves as a catalyst for new churches through the recruitment of local leaders, coaching and training of church leaders, and funding," according to the source I found. I'm fascinated by all things related to international cultures—food, politics, clothing, customs—so this ministry resonated with me.

I asked Michelle's husband, Tom, about working for Redeemer, since he had been its music director for seven years, and was encouraged by his response. Then I assessed the actual job, which required administration skills.

"Brian, should I try for this admin job at the church? Stop me if I'm going down a road I shouldn't be."

"You probably won't love the job," Brian responded, "but I'm sure you could do the work. You can do anything you set your mind to, including being a decent assistant. Give it a shot."

I applied and was called in for an interview. Pastor Gyger and another gentleman asked routine questions about my background and seemed excited when I mentioned the Billy Graham job. When I left the interview, I prayed again, more fervently.

Lord, if you don't want me to get this, please don't let them entertain the idea! I don't want to get into something that's not meant for me!

A few days later, the phone rang. "We'd love to have you as a Redeemer Presbyterian Church employee, working with the international division at their office on Madison Avenue in Midtown."

Wide-eyed and excited, I walked into the living room. "How ironic is this, Brian? I'm back working for another Christian nonprofit, something I couldn't believe I was doing the first time. And it's for the same church that gave us funds during 9/11! And the one we attend now! I just can't believe this turn of events."

"We could never have imagined a single one of the 'turn of events' that have happened to us since we both signed up for Match.com. The Lord moves in mysterious ways."

Brian bowed his head. "Lord, we thank you for all the blessings. We are humbled by all you do for us. Thank you, Lord!"

I settled into a routine at Redeemer and tried my best to conjure up the brain of an administrative assistant. The people I worked with were easy to get along with, and I enjoyed the office atmosphere. I felt blessed to have a job, even though it was clear from the start that the position called for skills that did not come easily to me. I tried hard every day, but I missed being a tour guide. Terribly. Leading groups around the City engages me in ways that sitting behind a computer in a small office can never do. In early March, I got a phone call from Junior Tours, a company that arranges tours for student groups.

"We have a weekend tour coming up with a public school from Mississippi on March 23 and 24. It's a standard itinerary. Would you be available?"

"Yes, I'll do it!" I screamed, totally losing any air of professionalism.

My first tour after 9/11 was with thirty-four high schoolers and five chaperones. As I looked at their itinerary, I noted that the typical "visit the World Trade Center Complex" had been replaced by "visit Ground Zero." As I came to terms with that, I suddenly realized I might be asked to share my story and had to consider what I might say. I decided to go with my feelings if the time came.

The weekend turned out to be miserable. The students and chaperones were plainly nervous about being in New York, and nothing I showed them or told them seemed to excite or interest them. I discovered that various roadblocks and security checkpoints made showing the city more challenging, both figuratively and literally.

When one of the chaperones pulled me aside privately and asked about my 9/11 experience, I opened up and told her the whole story, hoping it would help her warm up to me and the City. Later, I regretted sharing such personal information with her.

I took the group to the top of the Empire State Building but could not enjoy the view from the eighty-sixth floor because it was simply no comparison to the view from the World Trade Center observatory. I tried to remain positive, but privately I mourned the loss of that awesome view.

I thought I was ready for all this, but I guess I wasn't as prepared as I had hoped.

The visit to Ground Zero was particularly difficult. Panhandlers loudly recited facts about the death toll as they begged for money. Peddlers aggressively hawked books with gruesome photos from 9/11. Protesters displayed signs with outrageous conspiracy theories, blaming the US government or President Bush for the disaster. On the bus, a student asked about my 9/11 experience, and I said, "We lived Downtown and it was a big mess for us." End of story.

Although I tried to retain my chipper tour guide persona, the Ground Zero visit and the question left me shaky and anxious. As the students dispersed for free time in Times Square, I leaned against a pole and drank in the spectacle of "The Great White Way." The bright lights shining in Times Square seemed insipid set against the hell New Yorkers had just been through. Not to mention the pain that so many were still going through. It seemed like a deflection, an invalidation of the seriousness of what had just happened.

I wish these kids could have experienced the party of New York City before 9/11. All the attitude, the sights and sounds, the colorful people, the fun. But the City just isn't as fun now.

By the end of the weekend, I had to reevaluate whether I could continue to lead tours at all. I was afraid that traveling around the City and talking about 9/11 would trigger my PTSD or pull me back into depression. I decided that the only way I could continue to lead tours would be to change up my routine—although I wasn't sure what that would look like yet. And I vowed to deflect all questions about my personal experience on 9/11.

27

Hope and a Future

WHILE I WAS WORKING AT REDEEMER, Brian started interviewing for positions similar to those he had held before 9/11. But one evening he told me, "Christina, nothing feels right about any of these job interviews."

"What do you mean?" I responded. "Are you just in a funk? Is unemployment messing with your confidence? Don't be insecure, Brian. You'll find something! Remember, you're good at what you do!"

"It's not that I feel insecure—I'm just not excited about the jobs I'm interviewing for. I would've been interested in some of these positions in the past, but I just don't know how I feel about this kind of work anymore," he confessed. "I need to do some career soul-searching. I need to really pray about this," he said, becoming upset.

Brian seemed confused and concerned, and the conversation made me even more so.

Shouldn't he be taking any job he can get, no matter what it is? This isn't the time to pick and choose!

I shared my concerns about Brian with friend Michelle. "Brian is so qualified for so many upper management jobs in finance, computers, sales—he had a fabulous job making loads of money when he worked for IBM. I thought he liked what he did. Now he's saying the jobs he's been interviewing for 'no longer appeal to him.'"

"Maybe he just needs a break from the rat race to do something else," Michelle offered. "Heeeeeey, you know what? Redeemer has a job opening for an office manager. It might be a nice break for him to work at Redeemer."

I recoiled almost physically. "I hate that idea! Brian's on the corporate fast track! His entire adult journey had been dedicated to climbing the ladder. People love him in that world. They respect him. You should see them in that setting—he's great! He needs to do what he's good at. Not switch gears into the unknown."

Michelle shot me a look, and I remembered that her husband worked for Redeemer.

My worldly priorities had been challenged by 9/11, but I still craved the nice lifestyle that I expected Brian's career to provide for us. Even after all we had been through, was I still hoping for my Manhattan fairy-tale life, riding on my husband's high-profile, upper-class coattails? Yes, apparently I was. That dream would die like a block of ice on a hot road if he took this Redeemer job.

"Well, Christina, have you prayed about it? With Brian or alone?"

I got quiet. "Maybe I was just giving lip service when I told God I was ready to turn over control of my life. I guess that habit is dying hard. I mean, I *thought* I was ready to do that. But—this is asking a lot."

"Well, you need to give it up to God," Michelle exhorted. "And don't avoid praying about it because you're afraid of what the answer might be!"

I left the dinner frustrated and a little angry.

Still conflicted, the next day I approached Jerry, the receptionist at the Redeemer offices. Through clenched teeth, I asked, "Is the office manager position still open? If so, do you have a written job description?"

"Absolutely," he said, handing me the ad. "They need someone to fill the position right away. The church is growing so much right now that I know they are looking for someone with a business background."

That evening, I nonchalantly said, "Brian, there's a position available at Redeemer. I have the description if you're interested."

I was a little disappointed when he agreed to look at it.

He immediately started researching the position, applied for it, and then went on three successive interviews.

Each time, I secretly hoped he would say he didn't really want the position.

But every time, he responded, "I'm really thinking this sounds like a great fit for me! I'm excited about it!"

Three weeks after he first applied, Brian was offered the office manager position at Redeemer. But now it was his turn to soul-search.

"Christina, this would be a major life change for us," he said, looking into the distance as if he were talking to himself. "Do you know we'll be making much less than I made at IBM? Also, if I start work for a nonprofit, I might have to remain in that arena. Going between corporate and nonprofit work isn't as easy as you'd think. Sometimes corporations will pigeonhole a non-profit worker. I haven't worked for a nonprofit before, so now I have to think about whether I'd be OK working for one the rest of my career."

He continued, "I've never even taken religious courses. I might really be a fish out of water there."

"Let's pray about it," I said. "Lord, please let us know if you mean to move Brian in this direction. We're up for the challenge to move on in faith, and we're up for the challenge to re-examine what we thought was important. We're ready to change priorities. Thank you for this opportunity!"

The next morning, I said to Brian, "I feel strongly about this. I want you to take this job. I'm conflicted about it on one level, but that's my own stuff I've gotta work through. When it comes to you, something about it feels right. Just like something felt right about me taking the Redeemer Church Planting Center position."

Brian smiled. " I was going to tell you the same thing today."
Lord, please be in this decision. Please bless this. We want to serve
you. Send us where you want us.

⌒⌒⌒

Brian started at Redeemer, and I slowly began to get steady
tour work on the weekends as winter progressed into spring. I
learned new routes and changed up my patter that felt more comfortable to me and helped me show off the City I still loved. I so
badly wanted tourists to return—not just so myself and my fellow tour guides could return to work—but because it meant so
much for tourists to be here.

"You know, Brian, tourists coming to New York is so important. Tourism brings back a sense of normalcy for New Yorkers.
Visiting the City is the best thing people could do to help the
city get back onto its feet, don't ya think?"

Brian nodded. "And certainly, all tourists, especially American
tourists, need to visit Ground Zero. Christina, you have a great
opportunity to create awareness of 9/11 and connect visitors with
what happened that day and how it played out in the life of someone who experienced it. You really have a big role to play."

I smiled gratefully but didn't tell him that I rarely talked about
our personal experience on the tours. I felt I had to limit what I
said so that I could continue the tour without being depressed
or feeling exploited. Who wants a crying, irritable tour guide?

I knew I was missing an opportunity to help people understand
the full impact of the attacks by not telling my story, but I chose
to educate my tour groups in other ways. I scheduled generous
amounts of time at Ground Zero so they could really experience
the site and process the information I was giving them. There
were ever-changing platforms and overlooks as the pile was being
cleared, and I would get the groups as close to Ground Zero as
possible. And, if I *really* liked a group, I would bring them up to
my terrace and let them see it from that vantage point.

Those terrace visits also helped me to accept my new view. The "open wound" was healing—at Ground Zero and in my life. God used tour guiding to bring me healing, and I was so grateful for it.

In the fall, when it appeared that tourism was again robust enough for me to earn a full-time livelihood as a guide, I talked to Brian about quitting my job at Redeemer's Church Planting Center.

"The job filled the void, and I appreciate that and the income it has given me," I explained. "But I've learned a life lesson from this stint as an administrative assistant: 'I can do anything, but not everything.'"

No amount of effort on my part could make me good at the job. It made me exhausted and frustrated. "I tried my best, but there's value in learning what one is *not* good at."

Brian was understanding. "I agree. And I'm so glad you are returning to what you do best. It's funny—I'm the total opposite. I love my Redeemer job as much as you dislike yours. It's like I've been working there for forever."

He practically beamed. My husband was happy in a way I had not seen in a very long time.

"Yeah, I've noticed. Each morning you practically jump out of bed! This new frontier clearly is so right for you. It's your calling."

I thought silently for a few minutes and then said, "You know, Brian, maybe *I* was meant to work at the church just so I could open a door for *you* to work at the church."

He sat back on the sofa and smiled, then grabbed his Bible from the coffee table.

"I was just reminded of a passage in Jeremiah." He read, "'For I know the plans I have for you,' declares the Lord, 'plans to prosper you and not to harm you, plans to give you hope and a future. Then you will call on me and come and pray to me, and I will listen to you. You will seek me and find me when you seek me with all your heart.'"

Brian took my hand and prayed out loud. "Lord, thank you for those verses in Jeremiah. Thank you for bringing us to Redeemer. It's easy to see Redeemer was meant to play a huge role in our lives. And us in it."

28

Seeking Shalom for the City

In the Fall of 2002, I took Gaby on the now-reliable subway to Hell's Kitchen for a vet check-up. As we climbed the steps up to the street, I caught myself doing something I'd done ever since I moved to NYC: looking for the Twin Towers to give me a sense of direction.

The towers were so prominent in the skyline that they were visible within much of Manhattan, so if you got turned around on the Manhattan grid (very easy to do) all you had to do was look for the towers and *voila*—you could quickly determine which direction was north and south. But now the markers were gone. Realizing I had been looking for them reflexively, I became sad and wistful.

I miss those towers so much. Even if no one had been killed in the attacks, I would still be mourning the loss of the two buildings.

As I stood on the street, with Gaby sitting patiently at my feet, I contemplated how I was going to get my bearings now that the towers were gone. Just as tears welled up in my eyes, I experienced an epiphany.

Brian and I survived. Though we'll never forget, we are finding a "new normal" within this. And so are all New Yorkers. Even in the tiniest matter, like how we gauge directions. I have to be strong enough to accept a new direction, too.

I realized that other New Yorkers were coping too.

New Yorkers are a resilient breed who refuse to let terrorism keep them down. They've suffered a great loss, struggled, and are coming out the other side.

Even New York City itself was a survivor. I still loved New York City like it was a living being, but the being had changed. It had matured past its party phase and gotten wiser right in front of my eyes. It had endured and emerged out of the ashes like a champ, and I loved it for its resilience and how it was reinventing itself.

I used to show off the City in such a prideful way. "Look how cool this place is! Isn't it a gas? Don't you wish you lived here? You're missing the fun, this is where it's at."

Now I showed it off to my tour groups in ways that said, "Look at how strong this City is! Isn't it amazing how it has refused to stay down after such a terrible blow?"

A part of me would always grieve for the old New York, even as I appreciated what the City had accomplished. But standing on that street corner, I was suddenly certain that I would discover new methods to find my way—in the City streets and in my life.

The events on 9/11 stripped me down and broke apart my sense of self and my view of the world. God built me back up and left both Brian and me in a different place. God literally brought us from the ashes to a new life. A life with "hope and a future," just like Jeremiah prophesied. I called to God and prayed to him, and he listened to me. I found him when I sought him with my whole heart.

And I had a new goal related to the City too. Before 9/11, I wanted the City to serve me—to be a backdrop to my success. But things could never be the same after the terror attacks, and now I wanted to serve the City more than I wanted it to serve me. The goal had grown from a challenge I heard Tim Keller deliver to New York City Christians. He called us to "seek shalom of the city"—to work to bring peace and prosperity to the City and its people.

And in that sermon, Brian and I realized why we had felt called back to the City even after all that we experienced on 9/11, even when our apartment was still covered in dust and the streets were still filled with debris. God had brought us back here to "seek shalom" for this changed City. And Brian and I had every intention of doing just that.

Epilogue:
Never Forget

On September 12, 2011, the National September 11 Memorial opened to the public. The memorial, "Reflecting Absence," consists of two one-acre recessed pools in the exact footprints of the Twin Towers. The names of 2,983 victims of the attacks, including those who died in the planes, the Pentagon, the first responders, and those from the 1993 bombing, are inscribed on a wide barrier that surrounds the pools.

The victims' names are grouped together by shared connections, proximity at the time of the attacks, and company or organization affiliations. Jim White's name is listed next to his girlfriend, Amy O'Doherty. When I bring tour groups to the memorial, I tell them about Jim and Amy. I truly want to help tourists make the connection that names on the memorial represent real people.

I have my own title for the memorial. I call it "Endless Suffering," in deference to the family and friends who lost their loved ones on that day. The bottoms of the pools are not visible, which inspired my term.

The 9/11 Memorial Museum opened on May 21, 2014. The theme of the museum is "never forget," and if you go to the museum, you won't. I first visited the museum a month after it opened when one of my tour groups had extra tickets. Brian joined me, and we entered behind the group. We were directed to a room with TVs playing loops of news coverage from September 11. Seeing the horrified TV anchors struggle to inform viewers about the unbelievable events taking place took me right back to that day.

A separate room featured videos and photos depicting the boat evacuations. Brian and I looked closely but did not find images of ourselves in any of the pictures or videos. I wasn't expecting any, but it would have been meaningful to see a picture of ourselves in those life-altering moments. We continued through the exhibits quickly; neither of us was able to linger because the museum exhibits brought back too many emotions and memories.

I have been able to return for longer visits, however, and particularly appreciate the "In Memoriam" section, which displays pictures of all those who were killed and includes an audio loop that provides their profiles. Voices of relatives describe their loved one as family photos and a written description of the individual are projected onto a wall. The museum features 10,000 artifacts, 23,000 photographs, 1,900 oral histories, and 500 hours of film and video that help visitors truly grasp the scope of the attacks and the lost lives.

A quote I read within the museum sums up my feelings about that day: "As time has gone by it becomes less painful, but not less important."

Because of political struggles, financial problems, and legal squabbles among various parties, it took years and countless changes of plans before the memorial and museum were completed. It drove me crazy as a tour guide because I had to re-memorize every new plan in order to share it with tourists. After a while, I simply told tourists I wasn't up to date because I couldn't invest anymore memory cells into details of the rancorous drama. In the end, however, the bitter battles led to a beautiful memorial and museum that cultivate both memories and healing.

The lives that Brian and I have built in the years since 9/11 are in many ways like the memorial, which is beautiful and meaningful, even though it looks nothing like the towers it replaced. Very little has turned out as we expected when we got married, and our advances in life have often come after dramatic struggles. But we embrace our present place in life and are confident that we are where God wants us to be.

Redeemer Presbyterian Church remains a cornerstone in our lives, almost two decades after we first visited. Brian's office manager job quickly evolved into the position of chief financial officer. He manages over 100 employees who serve almost 6,000 congregants attending eight services in four locations. Brian was instrumental in transforming a former parking garage in Manhattan's Upper West Side into the "Redeemer West" location. It was a five-year project, and Brian considers its 2012 completion one of the most significant accomplishments of his life because it provides a place of worship for generations to come.

Brian also has been a key figure in the Jim White Memorial Golf Tournament, which is held annually before a Clemson home football game. The proceeds go toward scholarships for Clemson students, and more than $250,000 has been raised for the endowment.

In 2010, I returned to work at Redeemer as the coordinator of a short-term missions program, which has grown to fifteen trips per year to several different countries. Over 500 people have participated on these short-term teams, and I passionately want hundreds more to be involved in the future. I personally lead several trips every year, where I arrange the logistics, such as flights and accommodations; plan the projects, such as setting up medical clinics and teaching entrepreneurship initiatives; and lead a team to serve communities in countries such as Madagascar, South Africa, and Honduras. My passion for this work keeps in check my terrible fear of flying, which developed as a result of 9/11. Our teams care for the underrepresented and underserved within communities around the globe.

Because I have been on the receiving end of emergency aid, I feel I can serve others better and more genuinely. I am more aware of people who can't get help and what might be hindering them: fear of filling out forms to apply for help, no transportation, or maybe even no strength to get out of the house. When we do mission trips, we look for those folks. When I volunteer personally, I do the same. Because of our experiences on 9/11, I have developed a passion for the plight of the refugee. These people live long-term with the struggles Brian and I faced only for a short time.

We remained at 21 West for three more years and then decided to buy an apartment. Although we looked all over town, we settled on a building within a mile of 21 West. We had fallen too much in love with the Financial District to ever leave it. Today, we live just east of the new World Trade Center site, shaking our heads in disbelief as we watch the area change. New developments under way on the waterfront, the new South Street Seaport district, and FiDi's historic streets themselves will completely change the landscape of the Financial District. It's an exciting place to live.

Gabriel died of cancer in 2010. We loved that dog and miss him every day. Though he lived a normal Boston Terrier lifespan, we believe his ultimate demise was related to 9/11 because his cancer was rare.

My temporary break from acting became a permanent one as I never worked up the desire to return. I miss "the biz" sometimes, but look back with great fondness on my years as a performer. I still serve as a New York City tour guide, giving tours weekly—sometimes daily—and I still love it.

One of the lingering legacies of the World Trade Center collapse is health issues stemming from the toxins released in the air and in the dust that was ever-present for years afterward. By some reports, more than 2,500 toxins were included in the plume of ash-dust that coated Brian and me on 9/11, including cement, asbestos, carcinogens, fiberglass, pulverized building materials, electronic equipment, furniture, photographs, fingernails, bones, hair, and human tissue. Reports state that the toxicity of the debris was akin to that of drain cleaner.

These reports run counter to what we were told shortly after the attacks, when City and federal officials reassured us that the air and water were safe. In the years following 9/11, people started getting sick and dying, especially first responders and recovery workers who had worked on "the pile." The list of ailments related to 9/11 ash-dust now includes respiratory problems; various forms of cancer; and kidney, heart, liver, and nervous system deterioration. Some people got sick right away, but others have medical problems that took time to reveal themselves.

Although it's apparent to me that this situation was poorly handled, I reject conspiracy theories and try to believe that most errors occurred simply because 9/11 really was an unprecedented event. No one could have been prepared for all the long-term consequences, and Manhattan needed to recover quickly, for its sake and the country's sake. Personal responsibility also needs to be taken into account. Brian and I could have moved out of the area like others did. We didn't, and we are facing the consequences of that decision.

Today, I notice personal health problems that can't be explained away by natural aging or genetics, and I blame the dust. Though I would never claim to be a fitness nut, I did run the annual NYC marathon in 1996 and 1997, and as a tour guide I walk eight miles a day. But now I couldn't run a mile, I constantly cough, and those eight miles per day are getting harder and harder. Heart and lung tests have revealed no huge issues, but I was told that my lungs were probably scarred from 9/11. Brian and I weren't overcome by the dust and debris like the workers at the pile, but ours was a steady stream of exposure. Until the day we moved away from 21 West, we found dust in all crevices. And when we moved all our furniture to our new home, I was stunned to see just how much dust had been permanently there.

From that day, Brian and I have believed that we would die at a younger age than most of our peers, and we have noticed our health eroding more quickly than that of our contemporaries. It's like looking over the edge into the 9/11 memorial; no matter how hard we peer, the bottom is not visible, but we have made our peace with the uncertainty and believe God will call us home in his time.

For a death to be classified as a 9/11 homicide, evidence must show that any fatal illness was caused by exposure to the toxic dust on that day. Because their deaths fit those criteria, the names of several people who died more recently from exposure will be included in an additional World Trade Center memorial. It's being said that the real mass of 9/11 deaths is yet to come and that many names might be added to this new memorial. It's possible that our names could be added there as well.

My life has carried permanent imprints from that day, although it has been difficult over the years to discuss that day and its impact. Although I love my tour guide jobs, I still get uncomfortable when tourists ask me about my 9/11 story, and so I still tell it in the most general terms possible. The story is very personal, and it can still make me cry.

This book is my attempt at putting my story into words. I wanted to share the story—and my testimony of how God used 9/11 to transform Brian and me—with the world. I do not know whether my death will be recorded on any memorial that commemorates 9/11, although I'm certain my name is written in the Book of Life. I look forward to seeing my Savior when he calls me home—whenever that will be.

Made in the USA
Lexington, KY
11 September 2019